Vulnerability and Marginality in Human Services

Vulnerability has traditionally been conceived as a dichotomised status, where an individual by reason of a personal characteristic is classified as vulnerable or not. However, vulnerability is not static, and most, if not all, people are vulnerable at some time in their lives. Similarly, marginality is a social construct linked to power and control. Marginalised populations are relegated to the perimeters of power by legal and political structures and limited access to resources. Neither are fixed or essential categories.

This book draws on international research and scholarship related to these constructs, exploring vulnerability and marginality as they intersect with power and privilege. This exploration is undertaken through the lenses of intimacy and sexuality to consider vulnerability and marginality in the most personal of ways. This includes examining these concepts in relation to a range of professions, including social work, psychology, nursing, and allied health. A strong emphasis on the fluidity and complexity of vulnerability and marginality across cultures and at different times makes this a unique contribution to scholarship in this field.

This is essential reading for students and researchers involved with social work, social policy, sociology, and gender and sexuality studies.

Mark Henrickson is Associate Professor in the School of Social Work, Massey University, Auckland, New Zealand. His work experience and research interests are in HIV/AIDS and the communities that have been most heavily impacted by HIV: sexual and gender minorities, substance misusers, and the African diaspora.

Christa Fouché is Professor in the School of Counselling, Human Services and Social Work, University of Auckland, New Zealand. Her work experience and research interests are in HIV/AIDS, palliative care, chronic illness, and the organisational context of health and social service delivery.

Routledge Advances in Social Work

Vulnerability and Marginality in Human Services

Mark Henrickson and Christa Fouché

Routledge
Taylor & Francis Group

LONDON AND NEW YORK

First published 2017
by Routledge
2 Park Square, Milton Park, Abingdon, Oxon OX14 4RN

and by Routledge
711 Third Avenue, New York, NY 10017

Routledge is an imprint of the Taylor & Francis Group, an informa business

British Library Cataloging-in-Publication Data
A catalogue record for this book is available from the British Library

Library of Congress Cataloguing-in-Publication Data
Names: Henrickson, Mark, 1955– author. | Fouché, C. B. (Christa B.), author.
Title: Vulnerability and marginality in human service / Mark Henrickson
    and Christa Fouché.
Other titles: Routledge advances in social work.
Description: Abingdon, Oxon ; New York, NY : Routledge, 2017. |
    Series: Routledge advances in social work | Includes bibliographical
    references and index.
Identifiers: LCCN 2017003069 | ISBN 9781472476197 (hbk) |
    ISBN 9781315547855 (ebk)
Subjects: LCSH: Human services. | Marginality, Social. | Vulnerability
    (Personality trait) | Power (Social sciences) | MESH: Social Work—
    methods | Attitude of Health Personnel | Vulnerable Populations |
    Social Marginalization | Public Policy
Classification: LCC HV40 .H525 2017 | DDC 361—dc23
LC record available at https://lccn.loc.gov/2017003069

ISBN: 978-1-4724-7619-7 (hbk)
ISBN: 978-1-315-54785-5 (ebk)

Typeset in Times New Roman
by Apex CoVantage, LLC

Contents

Figures and table

Figures

Table

Acknowledgements

The authors are mindful of the privilege of the many conversations on vulnerability and marginality over the years with colleagues and students. These conversations have contributed to developing the ideas in this book. We are very grateful to both Val Sharpe and Ann Dupuis whose invaluable comments on early versions of the manuscript helped to refine our thinking and clarify our writing. We are also tremendously grateful to our families whose love and support (and tolerance of our absences) made this work possible. Thank you Jack, Marcel, and Maryke.

1 Why this book?

The purpose of this book is to explore vulnerability and marginality as they intersect with power and privilege. We will undertake this exploration through the lenses of intimacy and sexuality because these lenses allow us – in fact require us – to consider vulnerability and marginality in the most personal of ways. Vulnerability and marginality are words and concepts used routinely by politicians, researchers, and health and human service professionals around the world. We consider these concepts together because they are frequently used together to describe, label, and even create people at the social and economic margins of societies. These words are used by power elites to inform policy, and, as we argue, to manage and control those same people. These words are used popularly and even in the scholarly literature as though their meanings were obvious and shared. Yet vulnerability and marginality are complex ideas and, we will argue, largely created concepts. Neither vulnerability nor marginality is an *essential* category. These categories are socially constructed: that is, they are not biologically determined or innate to a person or family, but exist because of some shared social values or experiences within a culture, society, or economic system. Classifications of socially vulnerable and marginalised people vary from culture to culture, from time to time, and often from government to government over time within the same nation. Notions of vulnerability and marginality are constructed by shared social conventions, reinforced by popular discourse – for instance in popular and social media, business and civil society, religious institutions, and even gossip – and often by legislation, economic, and social policies and practices at the local, national, or international level. And of course different disciplines use the word 'vulnerable' in different ways: climate change scholars, for instance, understand vulnerable persons differently than do public health practitioners (Delor & Hubert, 2000), nurses (Aday, 2011), or social science researchers (Malagón-Oviedo & Czeresnia, 2015).

We are motivated to explore this topic and to write this book because of the ways we have seen the concepts of vulnerability and marginality being used and misused, particularly in nations where the gap between rich and poor – wealthy and 'vulnerable' – has become a dangerous social, economic, and political reality. We are very mindful of the dramatic increase in so-called marginalised people throughout the world: refugees and economic migrants; prisoners; people living in unimaginable poverty; people with socially stigmatised diseases and conditions; and ethnic, cultural, religious, sexual, and gender minorities. Too often in political and popular discourse the use of the language of vulnerability or marginality has become a way to label populations at the social and economic margins of societies and to create these labelled persons as 'others'. These labels dehumanise and construct persons as the negative sum of their deficits, often in moments of crises not of their own making. Such categorical labels ignore the strengths and resilience of individuals and communities, and not incidentally also ignore the complicity of political, social, and economic environments in creating vulnerable persons, and marginalising them. In this book, we challenge those labels, the process of labelling, and those with the power to label. We hope in a small way to advance a discourse of dignity, participation, and freedom.

This book is intended for people in helping roles and for those who educate them, in order to encourage awareness of the implications of the way we use the categorical labels of vulnerability and marginality, and to critique such simplistic taxonomy. If we accomplish nothing else with this book, we hope that we will encourage practice professionals to think critically about the way they use these words and concepts to describe and categorise their clients. This book is also intended for people who influence practice and social policy, such as social researchers, research ethicists, and agencies that fund research. Research with so-called vulnerable and marginalised persons is often considered too risky, too difficult, or too expensive, and vulnerable and marginalised people can be unnecessarily excluded from research, and their needs unknown, ignored, or even suppressed, often with the best of intentions, to 'protect' individuals from any hypothetical harm posed by researchers. Exclusion, we shall propose, creates more risk than the careful inclusion of so-called vulnerable and marginalised people in research. Two chapters of this book are specifically intended to highlight considerations for research with vulnerable and marginalised individuals and communities, and the ethical implications of such research.

It has been said (and attributed in various forms to Aristotle, Samuel Johnson, Gandhi, and others) that a society may be judged by the way it treats its most vulnerable members. There is little doubt that we, at least in the industrialised West (and to a lesser extent in emerging capitalist economies), are living in a neoliberal age where residualist notions of privatisation and profit prevail over institutionalist notions of social protection as a right. This attitude, in our view, puts a price on vulnerability and marginality, which increases rather than decreases the risk to the state. It certainly decreases choice and the quality of life of so-called vulnerable and marginalised persons, such as older persons in residential care. Mindful that the gloss is wearing thin off neoliberal claims, this book seeks to contribute to these discussions. We do not seek to contribute directly to the discourses of poverty and economic marginalisation because there are an ever-growing number of international economic experts in this area writing for other economists and policymakers; we want to speak with our colleagues, practitioners, and researchers who work at the coalface.

We as authors bring to this project our own experiences of vulnerability and marginality, and of working with and researching communities and persons who are labelled as vulnerable and marginalised. We recognise that to a certain extent we write from positions of privilege: we live in a society of laws and social protections; we are fed, sheltered, and educated; we are employed. These advantages do not disqualify us from the explorations found in this book, but rather impose an opportunity and an obligation to advocate for persons classified as vulnerable or marginalised, who, we shall suggest, could be anyone at any time. We also recognise that we may from time to time use the taxonomy of 'vulnerable' and 'marginalised' as categorical terms, which seems to contradict exactly the point we are trying to make. This is a limitation of language, and with these terms we mean 'anyone who is or has been or may be vulnerable or marginalised at any point in her, his, or their life'. We acknowledge the awkwardness of this phrasing, but it seems the best that English syntax can do.

In this book, we will consider concepts of vulnerability and marginality particularly through the lenses of intimacy and sexuality, which we will introduce further below. We have chosen this perspective in part because it is one with which we are most familiar, but mostly because these are the most personal arenas of an individual's life and allow us to consider vulnerability and marginality in the most personal of ways. There is no touch more intimate than the caress of a lover; we are never more emotionally vulnerable than when we meaningfully say 'I love you'. Intimacy and sexuality are the areas where we are most open to other people, and therefore the places where we are most at risk of being hurt and even abused by other people, including, unfortunately, professionals and other human services providers. We hear too often (and even once is too often) of cases of sexual abuse or violation where a physician, social worker, prison guard, or teacher has violated professional boundaries, misused their power and status, and sexually violated someone in their care. Consequently, intimacy and sexuality have become some of the most tightly regulated areas of human service work, in the name of protecting vulnerable persons. At the same time, older persons in residential care may rarely if ever be touched by anyone, and then only in the most clinical ways by their caregivers. They may long for the experience of a caring touch or a loving, intimate caress. Intimacy and sexuality are also areas that are highly regulated in every society, both formally and informally. They are areas where politicians and religious leaders delineate what constitutes morally and publicly acceptable expressions of gender and sexuality, and likewise, gossipers and religious and social leaders ensure that prevailing social norms and mores are enforced through labelling, social exclusion, and redemption.

Engaging the terms

In economically developed societies, vulnerability and marginality are overlapping but not synonymous categories: there are some people who are vulnerable who are not necessarily marginalised (such as a middle-class child with a life-threatening disease, or a wealthy businessman who has had a heart attack while playing golf), and some people who are marginalised who are not inherently vulnerable (such as political activists, or educated gay and lesbian people who demand full equality and legal protections within a society). However, in developed societies, there are some people who have been made both vulnerable and marginalised, such as homeless persons, people with substance misuse or addiction issues, the very poor who are also sick, people living with mental illnesses, and people living with HIV. This last group is particularly interesting and relevant for this discussion. People living with HIV are vulnerable because for the most part they rely on medications paid for or subsidised by governments (or insurers), but at the same time are marginalised in many cultures because of assumptions about how they became infected – that is, through some illegal or socially devalued sexual behaviours or relationships (whether or not this is true), or because they are poor. In some societies, diagnosis with HIV is itself *prima facie* evidence of a morally unacceptable lifestyle, even where the individual is living a life that fully conforms to dominant social mores.

Creating the other

Fundamental to these discourses in the 21st century is the presumption that vulnerable and marginalised persons are cultural *others*. From a historical perspective, this is a relatively recent presumption, which has been attributed to the rise of liberal humanism in the 16th and 17th centuries in European cultures (Harari, 2011). Liberal humanism emerged as the influence of the church waned and empirical science emerged as the dominant worldview. This worldview relocated the divine spirit from some numinous Other[1] that dwells above or beyond mortals to the individual. It holds that the sacred resides not 'out there', but rather within each and every human, and therefore individuals – rather than, or even in preference to, communities or societies – merit protection. This liberal notion runs counter to historical Western notions of how to treat the poor, which are founded in the so-called Deuteronomic Principle of Judaeo-Christian scripture. That principle was quite simple: if you do good (by being obedient to the laws, statutes, and ordinances of the numinous Other), you will be rewarded, and if you do evil (by being disobedient), you will be punished (see, for example, Deuteronomy 7:12, 28:1–22). Parents throughout the ages have used this principle to ensure good behaviour by their children: remember that Santa Claus *is* coming to town. To be rewarded was to be wealthy, healthy, and to have many children; to be punished was to be poor, sick, and childless. It was a short, if not logical, leap to assume that people who were wealthy, healthy, and had many children were particularly blessed, and therefore must be good people; and those who were poor, sick, and childless were being punished, and therefore must be bad people.[2] The Enlightenment Scottish moral philosopher and economist Adam Smith proposed that it was individual envy and admiration of the wealthy that formed the basis of both economics and a shared social morality. It is only when the poor annoy the wealthy or become a risk to public order that the state takes an interest in them. In the 1980s, for instance, we heard about children with HIV as the 'innocent victims' of AIDS, implying that other people with AIDS were guilty of something. It was the putative innocence of children, haemophiliacs, and faithful non-drug using partners with HIV who spurred legislatures into action in response to HIV, not the 'guilty victims' – gay men, injecting drug users, sex workers. In the simplistic Deuteronomic worldview, providing assistance to the poor was to interfere with divine justice. Despite the story of Job (and most of the New Testament), this Deuteronomic attitude seems to have informed Christianised Europe's practices and policies about poor, vulnerable, and marginalised

persons until the rise of liberal humanism. Indeed, the Deuteronomic attitude appears to be an underlying assumption of neoliberal economies even
today, where, as scholars like Rubin, Wacquant, and Higuchi maintain,
the neoliberal state punishes the poor for being poor by imprisoning them,
or highly regulating them with punitive practices short of incarceration
(Rubin, 2011; Wacquant, 2010), even if that poverty is the result of state
policies (Higuchi, 2004/2014).

Vulnerability

Liberal humanism, with roots in the European scientific revolution and
capitalism, was spread through imperial conquest and colonialism, and
ultimately imposed on or adopted by many non-European civilisations.
However, it is in European liberal humanist values that we find the origins
of professions like social work, which may explain why social work has
grown in countries more heavily influenced by European values (such as
the Nordic, English, and Spanish-speaking nations), and why it looks quite
different in countries less influenced by those values (such as East and
Southeast Asia). Liberal humanism and the construction of vulnerability
as a category have led to the siloing of legislation, funding, care and practice, and in research and ethical models. We in liberal humanist societies
now segregate people according to their perceived or socially constructed
vulnerability. Aday's seminal work in nursing, for instance, specifies vulnerable populations in America as high risk mothers and infants; chronically ill and disabled persons; persons living with HIV; mentally ill and
disabled persons; alcohol or substance abusers; suicide or homicide prone
persons; abusing families; homeless persons; and immigrants and refugees
(Aday, 2011, pp. 12–13). In other words, people are socially constructed as
vulnerable because of some inherent characteristic over which they have
little or no control yet require some kind of public response. The words
'vulnerable' and 'at risk' are often used by powerful elites interchangeably, with the implication that vulnerable persons are at risk for something
dire that will have negative consequences for their physical or emotional
wellbeing. Yet, as we shall suggest, it is the *status quo* of the state itself
and its control over the unruly poor that may be most at risk. In neoliberal
environments, we find a mix of the old Deuteronomic attitudes combined
with liberal humanism to create something of a pastiche of approaches to
vulnerable persons: if the individual is 'innocent' – that is, their vulnerability is not due to their own perceived failings – then they may have
access to more public assistance and sympathy. But if they are perceived

to be at fault, then they will be stigmatised and treated as sinners who must prove their value to society (by, for instance, working, or training to work).

Marginality

In some ways, 'the marginalised' are the shadow side of 'the vulnerable'. *Marginality* has been defined as "an involuntary position and condition of an individual or group at the margins of social, political, economic, ecological, and biophysical systems, that prevent them from access to resources, assets, services, restraining freedom of choice, preventing the development of capabilities, and eventually causing extreme poverty" (von Braun & Gatzweiler, 2014, p. 3). Exclusion is an indication of the extremely poor being at the margins of society, and in many cases, marginality is a root cause of poverty, and vice-versa. An obvious example of this construction of marginality is indigenous peoples who have been dispossessed from their traditional lands, customs, and traditions as a result of colonisation, government policies, and social attitudes, and who now endure a shocking proportion of social challenges in their post-colonial nations.[3] Marginality and social exclusion can be used synonymously. Marginalised persons and communities are relegated to the margins of cultures, nations, and global societies based on their perceived social value. People and communities who have characteristics that are less valued, or who are socially constructed as undesirable, inhabit the fringes of societies: this may be because of caste, religion, heritage, sexuality or gender, domicile, or occupation (such as the Dalit of India, the hijra of South Asia, funeral workers who handle dead bodies in East Asian cultures, drag queens, or homeless persons and sex workers in most cultures). Certainly most marginalised people are also in many ways vulnerable, particularly to poverty, illness, violence, and social exclusion.

Intimacy

Intimacy is one of those things, like art, where we may not be able to define it, but we know it when we see it, or at least when we experience it. On the most superficial level, intimacy has to do with close personal relationships. Intimacy involves a subject – the self – and an object – the other – an 'it' with whom the subject enters a relationship. We may enter into these proximate relationships with varying degrees of subjectivity, and eventually an 'it', which we encounter and classify through daily experiences, can, when we become truly human, and encounter the other as truly human, evolve into a 'Thou' (Buber, 1923/1937). Intimacy can be a body experience: "To become intimate with someone else, usually, tends to either be mediated through or focussed on the body" (Cole, 2014, p. 87). Certainly intense non-body intimacy can exist in genuinely celibate communities such as monasteries and convents, where souls are bared at the most profound level but there is no physical contact so that the intimate is not confused with the sexual. More recently, we might consider the kind of pseudo-intimacy found in social media, which may involve the disclosure of a great deal of personal information to a largely anonymous public audience, but here intimacy is rarely, if ever, reciprocated and mutual intimacy is at best unlikely. (That said, we are mindful of the array of dating and hook-up apps that have emerged to facilitate intimate contact between individuals, but these are a kind of marketplace intimacy that is an electronic heir to dance halls and discos, bars and pubs, and singles nights at selected grocery stores.)

Sexuality

Popularly, intimacy has become conflated, and is often used interchangeably with or as a Bowdlerised term for sexuality: a bodily experience of some kind of relationship however fleeting or enduring. Sexuality is different from intimacy, at least in the way we shall use this word here. Dunk-West and Hafford-Letchfield describe sexuality as an umbrella term that "relates to the private dimension in which people live out their sexual, intimate and/or emotional desires" (2011, p. 2). Sex can be the culmination of, and an ultimate expression of, intimacy, but it can also be degraded to being almost devoid of it. Common use of the concept of sexuality implies sexual behaviour, including penetrative intercourse and the array of fetishes and fantasies that fill human imaginations. But sexuality is also a concept that has come to mean something entirely separate from behaviour: identity. In contemporary discourse, and in this book, sexuality has to do with the way an individual understands themselves in the context of their anatomy, physical attraction to others (desire), and emotional attraction to others (falling in love). Occasionally, fantasies, including daydreams and night-time dreams, are included in this list, although we have discovered that this is not always relevant or useful, and can add to the confusion rather than the clarification of sexuality. All of these elements combine together in various ways to create something that is understood as sexual identity. Identity, then, is much more important than behaviours, and even relationships: it is a way an individual understands themselves as a whole person. This 'private dimension' also has a public dimension: as we shall explore in some detail in Chapter 3, some sexualities are valued more highly than others, depending on social, cultural, and political context, and the management of variant sexualities can range from indifference to public execution.

The focus and structure of this book

This book critiques and challenges the notion of objectively classifying people into 'the vulnerable' or 'the marginal'; instead it recognises that we can all be vulnerable and we can all be marginalised depending on the circumstances in which we find ourselves. A perfectly healthy middle-aged, middle-class politician walking down the street may suddenly be struck by a bus, and rendered unconscious. The status of that person changes from 'not vulnerable' to 'vulnerable' in an eyeblink, and that person is now entirely reliant on the kindness of strangers and whatever medical care system may respond. Likewise, a status of 'marginalised' may change according to circumstance or government policy: a well-educated or high-status person may choose to migrate with their family from one country to another to improve opportunities for their children; they may not speak the new language fluently, understand the health or political system, or find a job commensurate with their abilities because of racism, ethnocentrism, or xenophobia. That person has moved from 'not marginalised' to 'marginalised' because of their relocation to a different cultural context. Likewise, indigenous peoples who are forced by policy or circumstance to relocate from traditional lands to urban or non-traditional environments will experience a similar dislocation and reconceptualisation of self. States and elites such as religious authorities claim the power and privilege to manage the status of vulnerable and marginalised persons such as sexual or gender minorities: within a generation, for instance, in some countries, gay and lesbian people have moved from criminality to marriage equality, from the margins to the mainstream; in other countries, of course, they remain socially and legally very vulnerable to arrest, torture, violence, and death. This book asserts that vulnerability and marginality are fluid categories, and that they are layered categories: that is, there are many contributors to vulnerability and marginality, and different contributors may feature at different times and places because of the power claimed by privileged elites.

In the current neoliberal environment, social protection institutions and organisations have become risk-management and risk-averse organisations, driven by constructed notions of marginality and vulnerability. This approach fails to recognise that most individuals are highly resilient and capable of living meaningful lives and engaging in healthy and intimate relationships whatever their challenges or stage of life. In practice, risk aversion means that institutions that provide care can become manual-ised, highly regulated, problem-focussed environments with particular, binary constructions of gender and sexuality, which stifle resourcefulness and relationships. This in turn can mean that these institutions become warehouses of palliation and management of risk, rather than places that invite energy, life-enhancement, and reinvestment in living. Writing with a firm foothold in the liberal humanist tradition, we will propose in its place strength-based (Saleebey, 2002), salutogenic (Greene & Cohen, 2005), and negotiated care approaches (McCormack, 2003). These approaches focus on strengths, health, and possibilities, rather than deficits, and sup-port the discovery of meaningfulness in life at whatever age and with whatever ability. At the same time, negotiated care approaches recognise that resources are not unlimited, and that choices must be made by both client and care provider. Recognising that resources are limited does not imply that the care provider must simply accept resources as they are. Providers can and should advocate for the maximum possible resources to provide the best possible care. Nevertheless, resources will never be unlimited, and choices will always need to be made.

The shared background of the authors is social work, although we come to social work from very different contexts and experiences. Social work, however, has a values system that is, at least in theory, shared by all social workers around the world. These values include social change and devel-opment, social cohesion, empowerment and liberation of people, social justice, human rights, collective responsibility, and respect for diversities. Social work also draws on theoretical foundations in the social sciences, humanities, and indigenous communities as well as its own research and theoretical framework (International Association of Schools of Social Work & International Federation of Social Work, 2014). It is this con-text and these values that inform the framework and arguments of this book. In Chapter 2, we consider more carefully and in depth the concepts of vulnerability and marginality, and the social construction of these con-cepts. In Chapter 3, we will explore what we mean by intimacy and its more fraught sibling sexuality, and consider the contemporary construc-tion of diverse sexualities and genders as continua, rather than as more traditional either/or binaries. The very act of labelling someone as vulner-able or marginalised confers privilege, yet the nature of such privilege is such that it is difficult or impossible to conceptualise outside that privilege, or even to recognise that one is privileged. In Chapter 4, we will define the problems and challenges of power and privilege, particularly as found in neoliberal policy environments. Chapter 5 considers contexts of care, and considers in more depth the challenge of being problem or deficit-focussed. A deficit-focussed perspective results in vulnerable and marginalised persons themselves being problematised by practitioners and care workers who define them as vulnerable or marginalised. In Chapter 6, we consider alternatives to the challenge of risk-focussed care identified in Chapter 5; that is, to develop and explore human-centred approaches that build on individual and community strengths rather than on their labelled problems and 'deficits'. We will explore the notion that access to resources and power is not binary (you either have resources, or you do not), but sca-lar; that is, people have different access to different kinds of resources and power depending on circumstance and social and political context.

In Chapter 7, we turn our attention to research, and will examine the relationship between the researcher and individuals and communities that experience vulnerability and marginality. Challenges and strategies to engage with research participants, ethics committees, and other core stake-holders in designing research with vulnerable and marginalised popula-tions will be our focus in Chapter 8. In this chapter, we will raise questions about partnerships between communities, researchers, and ethical review committees, and consider unintentional harm that may be imposed in the processes designed to protect so-called vulnerable persons. And finally, in Chapter 9, we will consider ways to evaluate the claims that we make, and critique the currently dominant notions of accountability, effectiveness, and efficiency as desirable 'outcome' measures.

At the end of each chapter, we pose a series of key questions based on points in the chapter that can be used for individual reflection or discussion with communities of practice, study groups, or students. These questions pick up key themes in each chapter, and will be helpful for practition-ers who are undertaking continuing education as part of their professional development, or who participate in journal clubs, for advanced students who are part of study groups, or for educators and researchers facilitat-ing these discussions. The questions are intended to help initiate thought-ful discussions. Where such discussions go will, of course, be up to the participants!

It would be understating it to say that the development of this book has challenged our own notions of practice, research, and ethics, and we fully expect – and hope – that it will challenge readers. We do not need to be right about everything we propose, but we do hope to encourage readers to make more thoughtful and considered decisions. We expect that there will be points of controversy and even resistance, especially among practitioners and managers who have been trained to think of vulnerable and marginalised others as broken and powerless, and who therefore require management, and who also must respond to their policy masters in country capitals. Other readers may find themselves nodding in agreement. Our hope is that this book will encourage new thinking and creativity in the ways we as social workers and other human service providers, educators, and researchers conceptualise vulnerability, marginality, intimacy, and sexuality, and even in the ways we conceptualise ourselves.

Notes

1 Because of the limitation of language, we have ended up using the word 'other' in two ways. As we explain, the numinous 'Other' (with a capital O) is intended to refer to the divine power of the universe; 'other' with a lower case 'o' refers to people who are constructed as different, or less than, those who have the power to label them. It can be both noun and verb.

2 This notion, of course, ignores the rich literature of theodicy through the centuries, and particularly post Holocaust-Hiroshima, an exploration of which is beyond the scope of this discussion.

3 Definitions of 'indigenous' and 'poverty' are fungible. One major recent study suggests that although indigenous peoples constitute only about 5 percent of the global population, they make up 15 percent of the world's poor (Hall & Patrinos, 2012). In Australia, indigenous peoples (Aboriginal and Torres Strait Islanders) have markedly poorer indicators than the general population in infant mortality, child abuse and neglect, juvenile detention, education and employment, chronic diseases, suicide and youth suicide, and life expectancy and mortality (Australians Together, n.d., citing data from 2014). Native Americans have higher rates of poverty, poor housing, chronic disease, and youth suicide than the general population (NoiseCat, 2015). In Mexico, 72 percent of indigenous peoples live in extreme poverty (Underwood, 2014). On the other hand, while absolute numbers remain very large, of course, China seems to be making significant progress in improving the conditions of poverty among indigenous peoples (Hall & Patrinos, 2012).

Key questions for Chapter 1

We invite you to reflect on your position on some of the key issues raised in this chapter. Your answers may be quite different from our viewpoints – that is OK with us. The important thing is that each of us reflects critically on these issues.

As you begin this book, we invite you to reflect on how you have defined vulnerability and marginality in your practice or work.

- Who is a vulnerable person?
- Who is a marginalised person?
- What have you been taught, either formally or informally, about how to work with vulnerable and marginalised persons?
- How do you describe intimacy?
- How do you describe sexuality?
- To what extent do you think intimacy and sexuality should be considered in your professional practice with individuals?

2 Vulnerability and marginality

In the first chapter, we proposed that vulnerable and marginalised persons are constructed as cultural others – that is, that popular discourse, international agreements such as the Declaration of Helsinki (World Medical Association, 1964/2013), declarations such as the UNESCO Universal Declaration on Bioethics and Human Rights (2006), and occasionally country-specific legislation such as New Zealand's Vulnerable Children Act (2014) hold or imply that there is something ontologically different about vulnerable and marginalised people from everyone else. This is at variance with notions of vulnerability that hold that vulnerability is always contextual (e.g., Luna, 2009) and usually created. This chapter will consider a working understanding of vulnerability in practice and in research. We propose that vulnerability is not a class of persons, but a mutable, contextual, and layered construct that may apply to individual persons (and communities) from time to time, depending on circumstances and especially relationships. Nor, we propose, is vulnerability a durably definable characteristic of persons; it may change over time (Brown, 2014), and with fashions in economic and social policy. We suggest that the language of vulnerability has evolved into a category of persons because of policy and organisational convenience, and as a method of social control. It is easier and more expedient to talk about disempowered categories of persons rather than the messy business of individual persons with complex lives. However, some authors, particularly in the field of bioethics and medical research, argue that notions of vulnerability are appropriate for classes of persons (e.g., Hurst, 2008). We will consider the issue of resilience as the 'flip side' of vulnerability. Later in this chapter, we also consider contemporary understandings about marginality, which we propose again has to do with social control, and the ability – that is, the power – to label. Finally, this chapter will invite readers to examine their personal and professional attitudes about vulnerability and marginality in order to critique the sources of these attitudes and values, and explore ways to assess vulnerability and marginality as culturally constructed and an inherent characteristic of particular individuals at particular moments in time.

Vulnerability

Human vulnerability as a concept appears mostly in the social sciences, environmental, health, and ethical literature. The contemporary literature has proposed that vulnerability is not static, and that most, if not all, people are vulnerable in some way at some time in their lives (Martin, Tavaglione, & Hurst, 2014); indeed, vulnerability is inherent (Meek Lange, Rogers, & Dodds, 2013) to the essential human condition (Callahan, 2000; Kottow, 2003). Vulnerability has been described as the susceptibility to being harmed, and occurs at the intersection between threat and resilience (Adger, 2006). We will develop the concept of resilience more below. Humans are vulnerable by nature: our vulnerability is linked to having a physical body and being mortal (Gert, 2004). It is no coincidence that the powers of superheroes usually include invincibility – the antithesis of vulnerability – but frequently also include a singular point of vulnerability in order to make them more human. Disasters and catastrophes serve to highlight human frailty and vulnerability (Martin, Tavaglione, & Hurst, 2014). Writing from a climate-change perspective, Adger proposes that "Vulnerability is the degree to which a system is susceptible to and is unable to cope with adverse effects (of climate change)" (p. 269). In all formulations, the key parameters of human vulnerability are susceptibility, the stressors to which a system is exposed, the sensitivity of a system (or individual), and adaptive capacity. Thus, vulnerability research and resilience research have common elements of interest – the shocks and stresses experienced by the socio-ecological system, the response of the system or community, and the capacity for adaptive action in the interest of self by the individual, community, or system (Adger, 2006, p. 269).

In practice, "[Vulnerability] can operate as a gateway to extra assistance, but also as an entry point for social control" (Brown, 2014, p. 382). Identifying persons as vulnerable can lead to increased resources or protections (Fawcett, 2009; Finlayson, 2015), but can also lead to increased social control. Methods of social control can manifest by excluding or denying resources to people who are perceived as socially deviant, with the implication that only people who behave acceptably merit support and assistance. Brown (2014) has suggested that there is a 'vulnerability-transgression nexus' at the intersection between vulnerability and challenging and difficult behaviours, such as may be found in young people in state care who also exhibit so-called 'non-compliant' or transgressive behaviours. There may be a kind of artifice of vulnerability, where some people may take on the role of a vulnerable person in order to obtain access to additional resources, attention, or protection. To be sure, such 'false' vulnerability does not exclude the likelihood that there are very real vulnerabilities that exist below the veneer of transgression and tough behaviour, but these profound vulnerabilities are well protected and concealed. An artifice of vulnerability also suggests that even 'false' or 'pathogenic' vulnerability can manipulate authority and create a gateway to extra assistance, protection, or privileges (Meek Lange, Rogers, & Dodds, 2013). This extra assistance, however, will often come with the hidden hook of social control, where the individual must comply with the rules and regulations of those in power and authority, and so the vulnerability cycle may continue.

There are individuals and groups of people that everyone may agree are entirely vulnerable. This vulnerability is related to the ability to motivate, access, or take advantage of resources that they need, even if those resources are fully provided. An example of such a person is an infant, who is completely helpless and unable to motivate any resources in their environment; the infant is entirely at the mercy of the caregivers around them. We might say they are *absolutely* vulnerable. This kind of vulnerability can be transitional – an infant will grow to be an independent adult, for instance – or it may be permanent: a person may suffer permanent brain damage or be intellectually impaired, or unable to take care of themselves for their entire life. However, other than these special classes of persons, we propose that under conditions of unlimited resource, there would be no vulnerable people. What, then, about the refugee who is fleeing an unbearable conflict in their home country or region? Arguably, refugees, although often enduring unimaginable suffering, are at least able to do something for themselves; they may be victims of a gross injustice, but they have the ability to leave (even though this may be a dreadful option, but unlike the infant, they still can do something for themselves) and resettle. We might say that they are *relatively* vulnerable. What we notice here then is that vulnerability is scalar – there is a scale of ability to motivate, access, and take advantage of resources. Yet the more the individual accesses resources, the more the individual is vulnerable to social control. As we write, the greatest influx of refugees since World War II is moving across Europe, fleeing the conflicts brought about by religious sectarianism in the Middle East and South Asia. These refugees are enduring unimaginable hardship, but are still able to move from the conflicts in their homelands to seek refuge in more stable countries. Yet when these refugees enter the new states, they become subject to the states' limitations on the resources available to them, up to and including deportation back to their home countries. Vulnerability is a kind of constant bargain, then, between accessing resources and becoming subject to social control.

There are some economies that create contexts whereby 'vulnerable' individuals must behave in antisocial ways in order to gain access to resources. These economies and policy environments – our now-familiar nemesis neoliberalism, for instance – create the very kinds of behaviours that they attempt to prevent and punish. Arguments for labelling vulnerable and highly vulnerable persons have been called inadequate because they lack the notion of justice, including fairness in the distribution of goods and resources, which would address systematic oppression such as exploitation, marginalisation, powerlessness, cultural imperialism, and violence (Bamford, 2014, p. 39, citing Young). Such critiques argue that we should think of justice as involving the conditions necessary for the development and exercise of individual capacities, collective communication, and cooperation (Young, 1990), thereby ensuring that we promote values of social justice. There is, then, a connection between vulnerability and social and economic justice. People with equal access to resources and the ability to exercise that access are far less likely to be labelled as 'vulnerable' than people with less access. Access to resources is a matter of distributive justice, which is strongly associated with social justice.

We can see that vulnerability has everything to do with access to power and resources. If the power and resources (including my personal resilience) to which I have access are greater than the threat with which I am confronted, I am not vulnerable; if they are less than that threat, then I am vulnerable. If I need resources to which you have access, then in relation to you (and perhaps only in relation to you), I am vulnerable. If I need resources to which you have access and you require me to behave in a certain way in order to grant access, then you have made me vulnerable. If resources are denied to classes of people, then the power to deny those resources has created an injustice, and a class of vulnerable persons. The determination of vulnerability lies not with the individual or community under threat, but with those people in power who create justice, and control resources and access to those resources.

Vulnerability is not only not a binary status (vulnerable/invulnerable), it is layered (Luna, 2014): that is, there are multifarious contributors to vulnerability. Furthermore, an individual or community (or even a nation) may have multiple vulnerabilities, or at least have a variety of vulnerable facets to their lives. Vulnerability is manifest in specific places at specific times: the threshold between vulnerability and wellbeing is not the same for all sections of society, and because this threshold is based on values and preferences, it is institutionally and culturally determined and requires external judgments and interpretations (Adger, 2006, p. 276). I may have an intellectual impairment *and* a chronic life-threatening disease; I may be unemployed, lesbian, and physically disabled *and* require assistance in activities of daily living. I may not speak the dominant language *and* belong to a minority religion *and* have a physical disability; I may have just been the victim of a crime and have an intellectual impairment *and* be very old. But I also may be physically disabled and live in a society where access to all public facilities is mandatory, and therefore ramps and aids for the visually and hearing impaired are abundant. I may live in a society where anti-discrimination laws are so embedded that my being a lesbian is not noteworthy. I may have unimpeded access to health and home care, in which case what may have been significant vulnerabilities in one culture fall below the threshold of risk in the utopian society in which I find myself. In these ways, the complexity of vulnerability can be analysed, measured, and assessed (Delor & Hubert, 2000).

Likewise, we can also say that vulnerability is contextual: it is as much culturally constructed as it is an inherent characteristic of an individual at a moment in time. A person who is disempowered in one culture because of, say, their ethnicity, skin colour, age, or sexual identity may be highly valued in another for exactly those characteristics. Vulnerability is highly mutable, then, and contributors to vulnerability shift throughout an individual's life, as well as historically and culturally. Vulnerability is created when social institutions and helpers triage individuals because of actual or perceived limits on resources. By requiring unemployed persons to account for their time in socially valued ways (such as in work or education), governments seek to protect the finite resources of the national treasury; at the same time, by requiring all unemployed persons to work, they may be applying the template of less valued on persons who are physically, mentally, or otherwise unable to work. Governments also thereby place a value on certain kinds of work (such as manufacturing, agriculture, or IT consultant), and devalue other kinds of work (such as child rearing, caring for disabled family members, or doing the food shopping for the family).

The label of vulnerability is also used as an explanatory tool for referring to situations that suggest that these are not the 'fault' of the individual or group concerned. If I have been struck by a car driven by a drunk driver, or was born with a physical disability, I am in a class of vulnerable persons, even though I was not responsible for either of these things. There are moral connotations attached to the term 'vulnerable' and its potential to elicit sympathy; we may believe that children and the very old are vulnerable, and therefore should be offered special care and protection, although we may view a young adult with exactly the same intellectual and physical capacities in a less sympathetic way. If I was hit by a drunk driver, but I was also drunk at the time, even though I was 'vulnerable', less value is placed on my vulnerability because I will in some way be deemed culpable. How many times have we been told that someone has lung cancer, to which our first question is 'Did he smoke?', as though smoking somehow confers a kind of moral culpability, and therefore less vulnerability, to the smoker. Vulnerability has a strong paternalistic quality (Brown, 2014). If you label me as vulnerable, then you not only assume certain obligations over me to take care of me, you also assume certain rights to tell me how to behave, what my income should be, what life ambitions are and are not achievable, and so forth. Why would we find the achievement of Mark Inglis, the first double amputee to reach the summit of Mt Everest/ Chomolungma, so impressive if we did not believe it was not possible for him in the first place? While this achievement may be more an example of resilience and the ability to motivate resources, the fact that it was widely reported in the media suggests that it was perceived as the accomplishment of a vulnerable person.

Vulnerability and resilience

If vulnerability has to do with access to resources and the (in)ability to use those resources when confronted by threat, then vulnerability is linked with resilience. Resilience is variously defined, but in general has to do with the ability of an individual, organisation, or community to use resources to resile or spring back to its original form following an adverse stress. Resilience is a very complex topic (Liebenberg & Ungar, 2009; Windle, 2011), and a full exploration of the various aspects of resilience would take us down a rabbit hole that leads us far afield from the topics at hand. If an individual is particularly vulnerable to natural disasters – typhoons or severe erosion, say – but has access to sufficient resources and the ability to use those resources – strong building materials, or access to refuge – then the vulnerability to the environment is mitigated by those resources. If an individual is socially vulnerable, but has access to sufficient social support – such as a strong social network – then that social vulnerability is mitigated by those resources and the resilience of the individual's ability to use those resources.

In this way, we can conceptualise vulnerability as embedded in the construct of the ecology of the individual: the person in the context of their environment, and their ability to utilise the advantages of their environment in a resilient way. It has become axiomatic to say that during natural or anthropogenic disasters (such as crashes, explosions, and environmental degradation), it is the poor who suffer most: it is tautological to say that it is the poor who have the least access to resources, but in the context of discussions about resilience, it is important to restate it. People who are poor are most vulnerable to the effects of disaster because they have the least access to resources to cope with the disaster. Climate change and disaster experts now increasingly understand that social concepts of vulnerability and resilience are important in discussions of disasters. The people of Kiribati, a particularly low-lying Pacific atoll nation, are making plans to abandon their homeland because of the rising sea levels due to global climate change. Kiribati is not a rich nation by any means, and the people cannot afford to build taller structures: they can only plan to leave. The same can be said about people in socially vulnerable situations: a woman in an abusive relationship who does not have access to transportation, alternative accommodation, or legal support is much more vulnerable than a woman who has or is able to negotiate access to those resources; an injection drug user who is criminalised and denied access to sterile injecting equipment is much more vulnerable to arrest and disease than an injection drug user who lives in a legal environment where public health is prioritised over stigma about drug use. But simply because an individual is stigmatised, or even multiply stigmatised, does not mean that they are not resilient, as found by a study of African American sexual minority female sex workers in Florida, USA (Buttram, Surratt, & Kurtz, 2014).

Resilience, of course, has to do with psychosocial as well as economic resources. Since the emergence of strength-based perspectives and practice models (Saleebey, 2002), there has been a broad theoretical shift from a deficit perspective to the strengths perspective in the practices of many helping disciplines. Much resilience research has been done by developmental psychology in children and adolescents, but recently more work has considered resilience in specific population groups such as sexual minority adolescents (Gwadz et al., 2006), elders (Rosowsky, 2009), sexual minority elders (Butler, 2004), and people living with HIV (Poindexter & Shippy, 2008) to name but a few examples. Resilience research and practice recognises that given the opportunity and resources, even so-called vulnerable and marginalised individuals can address and overcome – or at least find a satisfactory way to live with – significant life challenges. Resilience recognises, for instance, that the 'problem' of sexual and gender minorities is not their sexual or gender minority status, but the cisgender heteronormative society or culture in which the minoritised individual lives; or that the challenge for older persons is not ageing, but the way ageing is perceived and constructed by professionals, institutions, and societies. This echoes the language of the disability rights movement of the 1960s and 1970s. In these ways, the environmental stressor is identified, and individuals, groups, and communities are encouraged to rediscover and live healthy, satisfactory lives. Resilience can also be exemplified in the response to the old psychoanalytic plaint about the origins of homosexuality: 'My mother made me a homosexual', to which the response was, 'If I gave her the wool, would she make me one too?' The second speaker's ironic adaptation of the pathologising language and the implication of hope is a clear demonstration of resilience.

Vulnerability and access to resources

We have seen that there is currently robust discussion and debate about the meaning of vulnerability in social services, environmental, and policy arenas. There is even more intense debate in the fields of bioethics, health research, and access to medical treatments. Bamford advocates for understandings that avoid vagueness, and justifies the ethical "pull" of vulnerability (2014, p. 38). When medical ethicists talk about 'vulnerable persons', they need to know exactly who they are talking about, particularly given the dreadful history of medical research such as in the Nazi concentration camps, which resulted in the Nuremburg Code (1949); the infamous Tuskegee experiment where prisoners with syphilis were left untreated to see what course the disease would take; forced sterilisations; forced abortions; and other ethical horrors. Researchers, funding bodies, and institutional review boards or human ethics committees now review all human and animal experiments to ensure that participants in those experiments are protected, and that (at least human) participation is completely informed and voluntary, and animal suffering kept to a minimum. Such committees have vulnerability-related obligations because vulnerability "is relevant to deciding what research is needed, when particular projects are merited, who should be recruited into research and how recruitment occurs, as well as to designing research" (Lange, Rogers, & Dodds, 2013, p. 334).

Health care providers are not only faced with the issue of defining, assessing, and managing vulnerability in research, but also in treatment (some of which may be related to research). Individuals who are particularly vulnerable are more likely to have their interests unjustly considered, and therefore should be afforded special protection in order to receive what is due everyone, but which they are less likely to receive (Martin, Tavaglione, & Hurst, 2014). Should people with intellectual disabilities, dementias, and mental health disorders have access to experimental cancer treatments? These individuals are often socially isolated, and may not fully understand the risks of such treatments (Witham, Beddow, & Haigh, 2015). Their capacity to consent is perceived by their health care providers as impaired, and therefore because of the lack of clear guidance, health care providers become gatekeepers to treatment based on their individual perceptions of vulnerability (Finlayson, 2015). Requiring fully informed consent to treatment could be understood as rendering such vulnerable persons even more vulnerable both to their disease process, and because the opportunity to consent may not be offered to them based on the judgment of another person (although a presumably informed professional). What are the balances of vulnerability in these cases? Ott (2014, p. 629) asserts that "the principle of respect for persons demands protection of those more vulnerable, not exclusion". One solution to this dilemma has been to reconstruct the issue of vulnerability from the ability to give consent (Schouten, 2015) to the concept of the avoidance of harm and the promotion of wellbeing.

Who is capable of understanding risk and making consent is a matter of great concern: traditionally and legally, parents make decisions for children up to a certain age, for instance, even though it is not the parents that will assume the greatest risk. But at what point is a child no longer vulnerable, or legally incompetent, but an individual endowed with the right to make decisions for themselves? The issue of transgender children highlights this question: who has the right to decide that a pre-adolescent child born with male anatomy but whose self-understanding is that she is female may start hormone treatments to defer puberty, and thus make gender transformation less physically onerous? At what point do adolescents with a chronic life-threatening disease have the right to make decisions for themselves to decline treatment, and even to end their lives? Do emancipated young people who have fled a violent home have the right to make decisions for themselves? Ott's observation seems equally apposite to these questions as much as to inclusion in research.

Questions about who is vulnerable and when someone is vulnerable are important for care providers, for in the current consent-driven environment, informed patient consent to treatment is paramount. If we have a significant medical treatment or surgical procedure, it is likely that a health care provider will sit down and have a serious conversation with us about the risks, benefits, and costs to the treatment, and we will probably have to sign a paper to indicate that we understand and give consent. We feel vulnerable at such moments because of the imbalance of information and experience, yet we are expected to participate actively in decisions about our own treatment. If we are unconscious, however, and are unable to consent to treatment and have not designated anyone to act for us, the health care provider is expected to act in our best interest. Yet despite the ritual around consent, we cannot give consent to every procedure. In most nations around the world, euthanasia or physician-assisted death are not legal even to end prolonged and agonising suffering, the outcome of which will be certain death. The wishes of even the most rational and clear-minded person about such a decision will not be respected; managing our own death is not considered in our own best interest. If we wish death, then we cannot possibly be in a right state of mind. The state draws a legal, if inconsistent, line around those things to which we may not consent. A variety of rationales may be offered in defence of states' positions on such matters, but they all can be reduced to the liberal humanist position that something sacred lies within each human. If we were to change our perspective about vulnerability and suggest that consent may not be the most important driver of health care decisions, but instead substituted something like 'our own best interest' or 'wellbeing', the decision framework might look considerably different.

Vulnerability is contextual and relational

In the way of these things, we believe contemporary notions of vulnerability are both/and: vulnerability is constructed both as contextual and inherent. Social work is relational; therefore, power relations occur within the context of a relationship. From a social work perspective that is firmly grounded in social and economic justice, we deplore the need for the notion of vulnerable populations, vulnerable people, or vulnerable persons as classes. Such classes of vulnerable persons are created by powerful entities and persons; an example of this is the new 'Ministry of Vulnerable Children/Oranga Tamariki' in Aotearoa New Zealand (Kenny, 2016), which name has been widely decried by social workers for all the reasons outlined in this chapter. Powerful entities create vulnerability by offering to protect classes of people from whom they have taken power. Neo-liberal governments concerned with conserving costs and managing risk are increasingly asserting power and control over resource-poor populations that increasingly have less voice and less ability to exercise their citizenship. The deinstitutionalisation in the 1970s and 1980s of persons diagnosed with mental illnesses is an example of this dynamic. Residents were discharged into communities, but communities were insufficiently resourced to provide appropriate care; suffering continued, but former inmates had the illusion of freedom and self-determination. People are notionally offered equal opportunities to be educated, to be healthy, but then are insufficiently resourced to succeed. Notions of vulnerability have been and are increasingly becoming codified, which is very concerning. Rather than endow these populations with more than merely access to resources, governments and power elites[1] manage risk by labelling them as vulnerable, then offering to protect them. This same principle is at work when there is money to be made by creating vulnerable classes of people: pharmaceutical companies define diseases (and thus vulnerable persons) in order to market solutions for sizable profit. It would seem that market-driven economies have the ability to create vulnerable populations. Can it be a coincidence that discourses of vulnerability have increased with the rise of neoliberalism and market economies? We acknowledge that vulnerability *qua sui* incurs no moral obligation, and that the obligation to provide justice to people who have less than their fair share of resources is a separate issue that derives from moral theory, not from a status of vulnerability (Martin, Tavaglione, & Hurst, 2014). Nevertheless, we believe that in practice, these two concepts are inextricably linked.

While notionally, concepts of vulnerability are both/and, considering both praxis and theoretical literature, we suggest that there is only one kind of vulnerability, which has to do with context and relationships. Vulnerability is relational: it is context-sensitive and context-dependent. Access to resources is the appropriate response to perceived vulnerability, not only increased protection (and therefore control). Access to resources by persons who have been labelled vulnerable will allow them to be more resilient, to participate more, and to require less protection. While it has been said that vulnerability and risk are two sides of the same coin (Beck, 2009), we challenge this notion; we propose rather that vulnerability and *resilience* are two sides of the same coin. For the most part (with the exception of 'absolutely vulnerable' persons, such as our newborn infant), it is the labell*ing* – the act of creating or applying the label – that creates the problem of vulnerability, not the label itself. At the same time, we have recognised that in practice, such labels can create pathways to access resources, or create contexts where social control can be traded for resources (such as the case of our refugee). We will explore this notion further in Chapter 6.

Marginality

Having considered a theoretical foundation for vulnerability, our consideration of marginality can proceed apace because many of the same conceptualisations will apply. Marginality was used early in English-language literature to describe a person between (that is, on the margins of) cultures (Park, 1928), but has now come more broadly to mean pushed away from the centre of a culture or group (Mohanty & Newhill, 2011). This conceptual change from *being between* to *being pushed* is significant in contemporary discussions of marginality. One of our questions in this section will be 'Who or what is doing the pushing?' Contemporary discourses about marginality weave together economic marginalisation, poverty, and social marginalisation that is experienced by stigmatised or by socially devalued minoritised groups. Considerations of marginality generally gravitate to one of these two camps, although in the social and cultural literature, there is not surprisingly a clear movement towards the latter. What these two conceptualisations have in common with each other, and with vulnerability, is that individuals and groups of people are marginalised by governments and other actors who have more power than they have. Power in this instance comes from legal, political, and socially valued standing (such as an ethnic, cultural, or linguistic majority), or simply from having greater access to resources and rights.

Poverty as marginalisation

Much of the marginalisation literature makes reference to poverty. Von Braun and Gatzweiler, who we met briefly in Chapter 1, suggest that marginality refers to where people are and to what they have. 'Where people are' refers not only to physical location, but also to social position; and 'what they have' refers to capital assets – using a broad definition of capital – and the rules and regulations (both formal and informal) that enable access to these assets (von Braun & Gatzweiler, 2014). If someone is poor, then they are prevented from participation in some, or most, of ordinary society, and their choices and personal capacities are severely limited: if a family of a young child cannot afford sport shoes, the child cannot participate in sports teams; if they cannot afford a computer, the child will fall behind in learning and in the basic skills necessary for the 21st century learner, which in turn will lead to reduced participation in higher learning and employment opportunities; if a parent cannot afford reliable child care, or transport, their employment opportunities will be severely limited, and so will their income, and the self-perpetuated spiral of poverty continues.

However, while poverty and exclusion are clearly related, it is not at all clear whether poverty leads to exclusion, exclusion leads to poverty, or whether there is some interaction of both that lead to social exclusion. "Being excluded, not only from growth but also from other dimensions of developmental and societal progress, is an indication of the extremely poor being at the margins of society and in many cases marginality is a root cause of poverty" (von Braun & Gatzweiler, 2014, p. 3). So then, if a transgender person has been marginalised by their culture, and education and employment opportunities are very limited, that person will then have a lower income, which leads to poverty and greater exclusion. In this instance, marginalisation has led to poverty.

Higuchi (2004/2014) writes that discourses that set out poverty as the only measure of marginality are too restrictive because they set out income as the sole indicator to address social exclusion. Contemporary neoliberal and residualist policies such as 'workfare' programmes that are intended to increase social participation by the extremely poor are predicated on economic understandings of marginalisation, which both blame people who rely on state welfare, but also attempt to address poverty through requiring or facilitating access to work. In economically difficult times, when state resources are constrained (such as the global financial crisis of 2007–08), states transfer their authority and responsibility for support of poor individuals and families to a plurality of actors, including private corporations, voluntary/not-for profits, and informal networks of families, friends, and neighbours. The involvement of these many actors changes the way social services operate. The state assumes that these other actors will take up more of the responsibility for 'managing' the poor, and the state can then cut its responsibility for welfare benefits and abandon its core responsibility to guarantee the basic living conditions of its people (Higuchi, 2004/2014).

However, it is not only economically difficult times that may lead the state to devolve its responsibility for poor and other marginalised persons.

The state may do so for reasons of philosophy or political expedience. Wacquant (2010, p. 202) sets out how this political process occurs: politicians find crime and poverty too troubling to manage by traditional means (such as rehabilitation or welfare), and set out new policies such as increased penal policies and more restrictive welfare policies. In order to make these new policies more acceptable, politicians characterize the socially marginal as undeserving and responsible for their own problems. This new characterisation convinces the public to accept and support the new policies, which are now seen as reasonable solutions to social marginality, and the policies are adopted. This is precisely the state of affairs many nations find themselves in today. Full prisons are a way of containing the socially marginalised, and cells are usually filled with the ethnically or culturally disadvantaged, minoritised, or otherwise marginalised persons in a society. States' management of deviance and marginality is increasingly punitive. We see a correlation between punitiveness in penal and welfare policies and practices across the mid- and late-20th century around the world. The correlation between marginality and imprisonment is by now considered 'firmly established' (Rubin, 2011, p. 201).

Marginality and social exclusion

Neoliberal approaches to poverty do not understand poverty as the intersection of a broader array of social exclusions. While poor people are certainly marginalised because they are excluded from society and participation in many social processes, they are only one part of the array of marginalised persons. Groups that are marginalised exist on the edges of social desirability and of our consciousness (Sue, 2010). Sue writes that to be confined to the margins is to be

> [O]ppressed, persecuted and subjugated; denied the rights of citizenship; imprisoned or entrapped in a lower standard of living; stripped of one's humanity and dignity; denied equal access and opportunity; invalidated of one's experiential reality; and restricted or limited as to life choices.
>
> (p. 6)

It is not poverty alone, then, but social exclusion more generally that demands our attention as we consider marginalisation. This refocussing leads us to a more multidimensional analysis of marginalisation. We must now consider the dynamic interaction of the marginalised individual's relationship to the state and to community. Conceptualising marginality as social exclusion both radicalises and expands our notions of marginality. Higuchi proposes that the introduction of the new political objective of social inclusion represents a change in social science and policy.

> As a result, it has become possible to argue that the appearance of social exclusion in contemporary society is not simply a recurrence of the problem of inequality but a new, catastrophic rupture.
>
> (Higuchi, 2004/2014, p. 114)

For Higuchi, this rupture is the decline of the Rousseauian model of the social contract, and the rise of a Hobbesian view of competition between individual interests that lies at the heart of neoliberalism.

Additional non-economic ways of marginalising are structured through laws (e.g., the criminalisation of same-gender relationships, or marriage equality), regulations (e.g., the banning of sexual relationships in residential aged care facilities), stigma (e.g., sex work, sexual minorities, or new migrants), or other social proscriptions (through religion or other social structures). Individuals are marginalised, then, because they belong to class(es) of people who are marginalised. Contemporary philosophers of marginality suggest that these two strands of marginality are joined together as governments create economic marginality (that is, poverty) through policy decisions and then punish the poor they create through carceral punishment because they are marginal (Wacquant, 2010).

Simply put, then, vulnerability and marginality are related in that they both have to do with access to power and resources.

It is clear by now that marginality is neither a simple nor straightforward concept: "'Marginality' is a multivocal category used in many narratives whose meanings shift according to who is speaking to whom, and in what context. It refers to physical space as well as a relationship" (Koc-Menard, 2015, p. 221). Marginalised populations must not be considered *ipso facto* vulnerable in all ways: the experiences of the AIDS activists (especially from queer communities) of the 1980s and early 1990s that disrupted public health, as well as medical and social care, empowered consumers of health care services, and resulted in a radical change in the way drug trials and experimental therapies were made available to people living with HIV (in the developed world) are evidence of the power that can be claimed by people who live on the margins.[2] Koc-Menard's work among the indigenous Quechua of Peru led her to understand how the Quechua claimed the derogated category of 'marginal' as a way of explaining their experiences of exclusion to the wider world. She further notes (citing Williams) that "'Marginality' is not only about domination and subordination. It is a complex hegemonic process better understood as a 'structure of feeling'" (p. 222). By this, she means that marginality can occur as part of a dialogic process, where one becomes aware of tensions that appear when one's own articulated experiences of marginality clash with experiences of another individual.

Frequently, marginalised communities claim marginalisation on the basis of culture, class, or condition: indigenous communities, for instance, may claim racism as a rationale for their exclusion from political discourse, and the concepts of ethnocentrism, heterosexism, homo- and transphobia, etc. are familiar ones. But Jönsson (2013, p. 165) suggests that framing problems in such a cultural way ('culturisation') creates more difficulties, and can often hide a critical discussion of the structural and institutional mechanisms behind marginalisation and social problems that are developed at the intersections of class, ethnicity, and gender among other power relations in society and at the global level. The response to marginalisation by culture usually calls for increased cultural competence and cultural diversity of the social workforce. However, cultural competence alone, while important in order to be able clearly to identify and articulate the claims of marginalised communities, is insufficient to resolve those claims. It is only by challenging notions of exclusion and power that such claims can truly, justly, and more permanently be resolved.

Marginality and the claims of citizenship

Such complex and multidimensional concepts of marginality lead us to the conceptualisation of citizenship. After all, if one is a citizen, one should expect to be able to participate fully in all aspects of society from the centre, not the margins. Concepts of modern citizenship are usually traced to the European Enlightenment period when states endowed individual citizens with rights. This understanding has been critiqued by feminists and postcolonial theorists who push understandings of citizenship beyond legal rights in order to consider the ways individuals encounter and engage with the state more broadly (Chopra, Williams, & Bhaskar, 2011). It is also critiqued by realists who recognise that the state can control its citizens by doling out rights and social welfare benefits to them. From their experience of Muslim artisans, Dalits, Tibetan exiles, and post-conflict Gujaratis, Chopra and colleagues suggest that citizenship is at the core of discussions about marginalisation, in which marginalised people view themselves as citizens, and how citizenship is lived experience operationalised through local practice. They propose that for marginalised communities, acts of protest and struggle functions as a primary mode through which citizenship claims become articulated and reworked (p. 244). This suggests that citizenship, and thus for our purposes, marginality, is always in a dynamic process of becoming realised, both for individuals and for societies. In the 21st century, of course, one of the urgent questions is whether and how rights to citizenship can be extended to migrants (Owen, 2013). As concepts of marginality are dynamic, so it seems concepts of citizenship must also be dynamic in an age when so many people throughout the world are displaced because of threats to life, opportunity, or prosperity.

As we proposed in our response to vulnerability, our response to marginality is not to 'help' the marginalised, but to critique power elites who create marginality. If marginalisation is involuntary, then it is the task of the social worker and other helping professionals voluntarily to inhabit the margins, and thereby to move the margins closer to the centre. An anti-marginal stance challenges the notion of marginality, which pushes people and communities to the margins. We will elaborate possible responses to marginality in the chapters that follow.

Notes

1 We use the term 'power elites' mindful of the historical use by C. Wright Mills (1956) in his work *The Power Elite*. In our use, these elites are persons with the political, social, or economic power to define, label, and control resources, either *de jure* or *de facto*. It does not imply that people outside these elite groups cannot challenge these labels.
2 Yet we must be mindful at the same time that many of these activists in the developed world were well-educated, highly articulate, and comparatively well-resourced in relation to many other HIV-affected persons in developing countries, or who inhabited multiply marginalised communities.

Key questions for Chapter 2

We believe that social work and other human service professionals and researchers need to critique our attitudes about vulnerability and marginality because, as we have seen, it is the powerful that create these categories, and put individuals into those categories.

- How do you define vulnerability? Which aspects of the proposed definition do you find challenging?
- How do you define marginality? Which aspects of the proposed definition do you find challenging?
- When have you experienced yourself as a vulnerable person? In what ways do you make others vulnerable?
- When have you been marginalised in your life? In what ways are you marginalised now? In what ways do you marginalise others?
- When have you professionally or personally been responsible for another person deemed 'vulnerable', or had to make an important decision for them?
- Do you think consent should be the paramount value in offering medical treatment to an individual?
- Do you think consent should be the paramount value in offering a social intervention to an individual?
- What rights does a homeless person have? How do you consider the right of a mentally ill homeless person to live on the streets? What about the right of a mentally ill person with a substance misuse problem to live on the streets? What about the right of a homeless woman with a dog to live on the street with the dog? How do we consider the rights of a homeless woman with a child to live on the street with the child?
- Who should be a citizen? What does 'citizen' mean?

3   Intimacy and sexuality

In the previous chapter, we explored vulnerability and marginality, the dual foci of this book. This chapter will consider the lenses through which we are considering vulnerability and marginality, namely intimacy and sexuality. We have chosen intimacy and sexuality as our lenses because they touch us at the deepest and most personal places of our lives. In order to consider these lenses, we must first review the taxonomy of these concepts because the language we use about intimacy, and particularly about sexuality, is very important. The language of sexuality in particular is evolving; historical and contemporary discourses about sexuality are inextricably linked with gender, although a full consideration of the language and construction of gender is beyond the scope of this book, and has been done by many others. As with vulnerability and marginality, we often use the words *intimacy* and *sexuality* in our personal and even our professional lives without seriously reflecting on what we mean by them. In this chapter, we align ourselves with current scholarship and encourage the reader to look beyond the historic discourses of sexual and gender binaries – that is, to go beyond the categories of male/female, hetero/homosexual and gay/straight, trans-/cisgender,[1] masculine/feminine, and so on – and to consider both sexuality and gender as continua rather than discrete categories, and ourselves and others as points on those continua who change with time and context. We explore some of the socio-political contexts that pose critical challenges to sexual and gender minorities, and why sexual and gender minorities in particular are marginalised and vulnerable. We consider theories of the aetiology of sexuality and how these theories have developed as responses to experiences of marginalisation. Finally, as a way of illustrating our point, we consider a population that has been marginalised and made vulnerable because of social and political constructions of intimacy and sexuality, that is, people living in residential care, and particularly ageing persons and people living with dementias. The management of intimacy and sexuality by law, policy, and regulation creates marginalised and vulnerable communities, and this in turn shapes how professionals treat people who are vulnerable and marginalised because they are sexual or gender minorities, and how we treat people in care.

If, as we will propose in a moment, sexuality and gender have to do with who we *are*, intimacy has to do with our *relationships*. The problem is immediately obvious: who we are is often defined by our relationships, not only by ourselves but also by the societies and cultures in which we live. If I am a man who is sexually active with another man, many people would identify me as 'gay', but I may also be in an intimate relationship with a woman, and not identify myself as gay, or even 'bisexual' (Ward, 2015). Persons with negative judgments about gay people will attribute a variety of stigmatising labels to me because I am in a relationship with a man (sinner, pervert, or criminal); gay people will focus on my relationship with a woman and attribute a variety of other negative labels (deceitful, 'in denial', closet queen). Yet I may be simply, at different moments in time, in intimate, perhaps sexual, relationships with people of different genders. I may even understand myself as gender variant. If I was assigned the male gender at birth, but understand myself as female, and I am sexually active with a man, does that make me gay because of my plumbing? Or straight because of how I understand myself? Or if I am married to a woman, does that make me lesbian because of how I understand my gender? How I understand myself may or may not be consonant with how I am identified by others. Do I have the right to define myself? Or must I always be defined, and perhaps confined, by the understandings and categories of others? Do I have an obligation to conform to the social norms and categories of the society in which I live, even at the cost to my own sense of identity and integrity? The answers to these questions will depend not only on my internal, personal answers, but also on the cultural values with which I was raised, and the cultural context in which I live. Furthermore, as we shall see, the state (perhaps as a mirror of dominant social attitudes) often inserts itself into this identity process, providing legal sanction for and against certain kinds of behaviours, relationships, and gender presentations. We must ask, of course, whether this is an appropriate role for the state. Intimacy, sexuality, and gender together with individuals, societies, and states form a complex multidimensional matrix that every person must negotiate every moment of their lives.

Taxonomy

Before we continue, it will be useful to survey the landscape of the language in this area. This is a dangerous undertaking because the vocabulary is as dynamic as the people it attempts to describe, and words and concepts change according to both the speaker and the audience. There are also 'insider' terms, which are not appropriately used by people who are not members of the communities or groups in question. Activists may use words that researchers and clinicians are slower to adopt. It is, of course, for researchers, clinicians, ethicists, policymakers, and others to use the vocabulary and syntax that individuals use about themselves, but there is disagreement even (or perhaps especially!) among people who write and talk frequently about sexual and gender identities, and who live those identities. The language of sexuality and gender identity is unsettled at the moment, and probably will be so for some time. The dynamism of language reflects how dynamic these concepts and identities have become. We acknowledge therefore that there will be people who will disagree – perhaps strongly – with what we summarise here. However, we are not attempting an exhaustive etymology: that is done better by others. Here our purpose is to introduce the complexity of using concepts of intimacy and sexuality, and to explain the language that we will use. In practice, we stand by two enduring principles: (1) if you cannot figure out whether someone is male, female, or gender variant, or if they are gay, straight, or in-between, ask yourself if it really matters; and (2) if it really matters and if you are in doubt about how to refer to someone, ask them. You will not be the first person to ask. In fact, the BBC has reported that there is a contemporary movement among university students to include preferred pronouns on name tags and introductions (Chak, 2015). Whether this is an enduring trend remains to be seen.

Language is important, and not only describes but also shapes identities. Historians such as Jonathan Ned Katz (1996/2007), Jeffery Weeks (2009), and Hanne Blank (2012) have thoroughly explored the sources and development of much of our contemporary language about sexuality, and it is not our purpose to reproduce their excellent work here. However, a brief overview may be useful for readers who are not familiar with this complex history. The words 'homosexual' and 'heterosexual' (hybrids of Greek and Latin roots) first appeared in print as adjectives in German in Krafft-Ebing's *Psychopathia Sexualis* published in 1886, and in English in Chaddock's 1892 translation; alternative terms for 'homosexual' (notably 'sexual invert', 'uranian') were also in use at the time, but were not widely adopted. (The word 'homosexual' as adjective, and certainly as a noun, is now considered quite dated, and is rarely used in the scholarly community, although it is often used pejoratively by hostile politicians.) However, it is clear that same-sex attraction (if not identities) have existed in all cultures throughout history (see, for instance, Boellstorff, 2005; Crompton, 2003; Epprecht, 2008; Leupp, 1997; Martin, Jackson, McLelland, & Yue, 2008; Murray, 2002; Murray & Roscoe, 1997; Sang, 2003; Vanita, 2002; Vitiello, 2011, among many others).

The concept of a 'heterosexual' person was first used by Karl Ulrichs (in 1862) and Karl-Maria Kertbeny (in 1868), who coined the word as part of their opposition to Paragraph 143 of the Prussian Penal Code (of 1851), which prescribed harsh punishments for anyone convicted of "unnatural fornication between people and animals as well as between persons of the male sex" (Blank, 2012, p. 16). Contemporary concepts of sexual identity, therefore, have their roots in protest against perceived injustice and legal sanctions against specific minoritised sexual behaviours. However, even 'heterosexual' in its 19th century usage had a pathologising aspect to it because it meant someone who was abnormally obsessed with the opposite sex – that is, someone (male or female) who desired sex with an opposite sex partner without the larger purpose of procreation (Blank, 2012; Katz, 1996/2007). 'Heterosexual' did not appear in print in its more modern usage until the 1930s when it came to define, and be defined as, 'normal' sexuality. This reconceptualisation was extremely important because it was only at this point that non-heterosexual behaviour was reconceptualised as 'abnormal' (Ward, 2015). Even today, "there seems to be no aspect of 'heterosexual' for which a truly iron-clad definition has been established" (Blank, 2012, p. xix). All of these concepts and words were culturally constructed, arguably created categories of persons that had not previously existed as such, and had their roots in opposition to legal control. Ulrichs and Kertbeny were not successful in their protest: Paragraph 143 was not repealed until 1969, and was used by the Nazis as a rationale to legitimise the incarceration and murder of homosexuals in concentration camps during World War II (Blank, 2012).

Contemporary Western notions of identity are reflected in English language labels such as gay, lesbian, bisexual, trans*, intersex, and so forth, but in many cultures, such essentialised and individuated categories have no meaning, and there are cultures and languages with more than two gender signifiers, such as the *bissu* of Sulawesi, Indonesia. Table 3.1 is a sampling of some of the vocabulary used for sexual and gender minorities in some cultures around the world. Recently, an asterisk has been added by

Table 3.1 A sampling of cultural vocabularies of sexual and gender minorities

Aikāne (Hawai'i)	Lai cai (Vietnam)	Supik-jantan, tom-boi
'Akavaine (Cook	Lakín-on (Philippines ♀)	(Indonesia ♀)
Islands)	[Faka-]Leiti (Tonga)*	T, Bo (Chinese Taipei)
Bakla, bantut, bayot	Māhu (Tahiti)	Takatāpui (Māori)
(Philippines ♂)	Mak nyah (Malaysia)	Tongzhi (PR China)
Bujang-gadis, becong	Maotoane (Sesotho)	Umbunkotshani
(Indonesia ♂)	'Miss July' (Kiribati)	(Ndebele)
Esenge (Ovambo)	[from i-Kiribati	Wadna (Fiji)
Fa'fafine (Samoa)	Independence Day]	Woubi, oubi, ibbi
Hijra (India)	Nkoshana (Zulu)	(Wolof)
Hungochani (Shona)	Pinapinaaine (Tuvalu)	Xanith (Oman)
Kathoey (Thailand)	Raerae (Cook Islands)	'Yan daudu (Hausa)
Kuchi (E. Africa)		

some people to the prefix 'trans*' to indicate that it is a word that includes many possible suffixes (paralleling search engine techniques); however, this asterisk is itself contested by some activists who contend that 'trans' (meaning someone whose self-identity is different to the gender to which they were assigned at birth) is sufficiently inclusive of itself to transcend categories. The opposite of transgender, of course, is cisgender, a word that was coined to mean someone whose self-identity is consistent with the gender to which they were assigned at birth. Whether to use 'transgender' or 'transgendered' (and, of course, cisgender or cisgendered) remains contested. Binary and categorical identities have been replaced by contemporary understandings of sexualities and genders as multidimensional continua (Teich, 2012), resulting in matrices of identities (Figure 3.1).

'Intersex' is a word that itself has a multiplicity of meanings; it means located between 'male' and female', but in contemporary use, it may mean *both* male and female, or *neither* male nor female, or a number of different things in between. Intersex identities can range from a cultural choice about gender presentation to the more dated term 'hermaphrodite', which includes a variety of genetic aetiologies and expressions (Cornwall, 2010; Feder, 2014), including people carrying the XXY sex-chromosome anomaly (known as Kleinfelter Syndrome), which is estimated to affect one in every 2,000 people assigned as male at birth (Blank, 2012). Here we can but acknowledge that this word and identity exists, and is, now unsurprisingly, complex.

Other vocabulary in this domain includes the word 'queer', used by some insiders to underscore the outsider nature of sexual and gender minorities, to reclaim a term of bullying and hate, to align with the contemporary

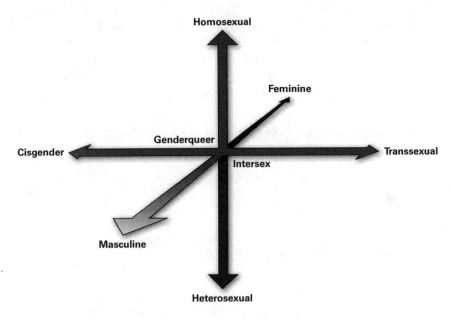

Figure 3.1 A three-dimensional matrix of sexual and gender identity.

scholarships of queer theory, and to highlight the multiple English language meanings of queer; like most of these terms, it does not translate well into non-English languages. 'Questioning' (another 'Q') is often used to describe people who have not worked it all out yet, or who are unwilling to pin a label on themselves. None of these identity categories imply anything about the behaviours or romantic attractions of people. Public health has coined the rather awkward language of 'men who have sex with men' (MSM), 'men who have sex with men and women' (MSMW), WSW, and so forth in an attempt to describe sexual behaviour in the context of behavioural risk. Some progressive social services agencies have adopted the language of 'same-sex attracted' in well-meaning attempts to be inclusive at intake. These attempts still effectively essentialise what are fluid and dynamic behaviours and attractions. Furthermore, they are inevitably abbreviated into acronyms (SSA, or 'same sex attracted'), which, along with LGBTIQQ, etc., attempt to be inclusive, and in the attempt just as inevitably exclude someone or some group, particularly in multicultural contexts. Some global authorities have more recently added the language 'Sexual Orientation Gender Identity, and Gender Expression' (SOGIE) to refer to these minority groups, but surely every person has a sexual orientation, gender identity, and gender expression (even if they are fluid), and so we find this language again replicates majority understandings of 'othered' identities.

Current academic writing uses the inclusive language 'sexual and gender minorities' (which we will not abbreviate) as an attempt to reflect the broad scope of these concepts, and that is the language that we will use for the most part. 'Minorities' here reflects a statistical concept, but also the reality that sexual and gender minorities are currently, and for the foreseeable future, minoritised by the people with the power to define, and more importantly to enforce, what is currently 'normal'.

Heteronormativity

It is the contemporary dominance of heterosexuality and its socio-political context that constructs minoritised sexual and gender identities as unusual or variant. This socio-political context is called *heteronormativity*, the assumption that heterosexuality, and its accompanying rights, institutions, and privileges (including reproduction and the right to raise children) is natural, inevitable, or desirable (Kitzinger, 2005; Montgomery & Stewart, 2012). Heteronormativity is different from heterosexual privilege (Feigenbaum, 2007) in that the latter specifically relates to privileges accrued to sexual and gender majorities by virtue of their majority status; these privileges include choices in behaviour, and legal and political rights. Heteronormativity assumes that heterosexuality is normal and standard (as we saw above), and implicitly and explicitly writes it into the laws of many nations and states. The assumptions include, for instance, that opposite-sex marriage was somehow divinely instituted, and remained intact and consistent for all socioeconomic classes of people throughout human history; that normal families require both (and only) a mother and father; that certain kinds of consensual sexual behaviour are criminal; and are all rooted in heteronormativity. Heteronormativity inevitably constructs gender and sexual minorities as marginalised and vulnerable. The contemporary management of sexual and gender minorities with arrest, incarceration, shock treatment, physical and chemical castration and state-sanctioned torture, and death by stoning, hanging, or being thrown from tall buildings are examples of how the states and quasi states have controlled, and continue to control, sexual and gender minorities (Fone, 2000). Ironically, however, many anti-sodomy and anti-homosexual laws exist in post-colonial nations, making heteronormativity an enduring colonial legacy. One recent report (Kaleidoscope Trust, 2015), for instance, found that over 90 percent of citizens of British Commonwealth nations live in a jurisdiction that continues to criminalise sexual and gender minorities, despite the 2012 Commonwealth Charter's aspiration to the "protection and promotion of civil, political, economic, social and cultural rights, including the right to development, for all without discrimination on any grounds" (Commonwealth Heads of Government, 2012, p. 3). Indeed, British colonial anti-homosexual laws appear particularly in South Asia, Africa, and the Caribbean (Aldrich, 2003; Lennox et al., 2013), even after independence (see, for instance, Section 377 of the Indian Penal Code, which criminalises sexual activity 'against the order of nature'; nature, presumably, being a heterosexual man). Although she was speaking of lesbian women, Adrienne Rich, the late American poet, could have been speaking of all sexual and gender minorities when she wrote "Heterosexuality has had to be imposed, managed, organized propagandized and maintained by force" (1980/1986, p. 50).

These realities make self-identification and public disclosure, or 'coming out', as a sexual or gender minoritised person hardly a taken-for-granted step, but an act of great courage and integrity, and in some nations, great personal risk. Acknowledgement of one's sexual or gender minority status also requires resituating oneself in the context of one's cultural norms, and this, in turn, creates the opportunity to help critique and redefine one's culture. It is for these reasons that we consider sexual and gender minorities as particularly marginalised and vulnerable groups as we defined them in Chapter 2.

Intimacy

Contemporary intimacy is a contested concept, and scholars, poets, and musicians alike struggle to define it. We certainly recognise the lack of intimacy in our lives when we feel lonely or isolated, but it is more difficult to identify when we have achieved satisfactory, fulfilling intimacy. The difficulty in defining intimacy comes in part because intimacy has not only become an arena of multiplicity, but its social, ethical, and political meaning is indeterminate and contested (Frank, Clough, & Seidman, 2013, p. 2). "Intimacy increasingly suggests an ongoing process of self and other subjective exploration and mutual self-revelation in a quest to be authentic and forge a rich intimate solidarity" (Frank, Clough, & Seidman, 2013, p. 3). In other words, it is complicated.

An important aspect of human intimacy is that it is relational: intimacy is something that occurs in the context of some kind of relationship with someone (or something), and these intimate relationships can take an almost infinite variety of forms, including the parental and the sibling, the romantic and the erotic, the long term and the brief, the transactional and the altruistic, the physical and the metaphysical, or even baby and binky. Although some theorists (Cole, 2014) hold that intimacy usually involves, or even requires, a body, this is only one kind of interpersonal intimacy; contemporary intimacy can occur virtually, via social media for instance, as well as in person (Nicholson, 2013; Scott, Mottarella, & Lavooy, 2006). We may find ourselves posting quite personal thoughts and revelations on what are essentially public, permanent forums, engaging in new ways in order to invite connection with our most private selves. This suggests that intimacy is more than just a 'nice to have' part of our lives: it suggests that intimacy is a fundamental need in most human lives, a need that goes beyond mere pair-bonding, and has to do with the experience of belonging. Seidman (2013) proposes that intimacy is the chief staging ground to realise an authentic path to self-fulfilment along with a secure sense of belonging. Intimacy compels selves "to share their innermost interior lives and to explore depths of emotional, psychic openness and connection; it demands an empathic, trusting self for whom the sharing of one's inner life is to be treated as a sacred trust" (p. 21). Intimacy is a sacred space that is located at the very heart of who we are as human beings. To invite someone into that space is to risk vulnerability, for there is always the possibility that what we offer will not be accepted.

Intimacy always occurs in cultural, social, and even political contexts (Mackenzie, 2013), and those contexts are inescapable. So thoroughly are we indoctrinated into those contexts that we must work hard even to become aware of them, let alone to escape them. Our intimate worlds are situated in the contexts of race, class, heteronormativity, and gender. These contexts shape not only the opportunities but also the content and boundaries of intimacy (Emens, 2009). These boundaries are established and enforced by cultures, societies, religions, and states. As long as states license marriages (or their equivalents), this private intimacy is publicly regulated; as long as states confer advantages to particular categories of persons, then those who fall outside those categories are made vulnerable because they are excluded from certain state-sanctioned benefits (such as property rights, inheritance, routine decision-making authority, etc.), and this exclusion has what Emens (2009, p. 1310) calls welfare consequences. We do not have to look very far back in history to discover state anti-miscegenation laws that enforced homogamy (marriage within type, class, or race) by prohibiting marriage between two people of different races, anti-sodomy laws, or even Downton Abbey-style cultural anguish about landed gentry marrying out of their social and economic class; or to find contemporary states and religions that ban same-sex marriage, or refuse to recognise intimate and sexual relationships between certain classes of people. Yet states have increasingly changed their approaches to contested areas of intimacy such as reproduction and contraception, cohabitation, divorce and remarriage, single (and even multiple) parenthood, sex work, homosexuality, transgender persons, etc. Nevertheless, the history of marriage seems full of contradictions, including the early Christian church's endorsement and blessing of same-sex unions (Boswell, 1995). At this writing, at least twenty nations have recognised marriage equality (Netherlands, Belgium, Spain, Canada, South Africa, Norway, Sweden, Portugal, Iceland, Argentina, Denmark, Brazil, France, Uruguay, Aotearoa New Zealand, United Kingdom, Luxembourg, United States, Ireland, and Finland; some parts of Mexico also license same-sex marriages). While some religions around the world remain strongly opposed to same-sex marriage (such as the Roman Catholic Church, the Latter Day Saints, Orthodox Jews, Islam), others have moved to recognition (such as the Presbyterian Church in the USA, Unitarians Universalists, Conservative Jews, Evangelical Lutherans in the USA, the Anglican Church of Canada, and the Episcopal Church in the USA, although some other churches in the Anglican Communion remain committed to opposing marriage equality). Marriage, of course, is not the only place where states exercise regulatory control of intimacy, but it is an illustrative one. The role of authoritative institutions such as the state and religion has evolved along with conceptualisations of personhood, human rights, and even marriage. Importantly, it may not even be legal marriage that contemporary same-sex couples seek, but the *right* to marry legally (Henrickson, 2010). From scripted relationships, contemporary companionate relationships have evolved into something more self-determined, which is gradually, and perhaps inevitably, being recognised by states and religions. Frank, Clough, and Seidman (2013) propose that we are moving into a post marital era, one of "intimate citizenship", where selves have a right to personal intimate freedom with regard to partner selection, the social form of intimacy, and the way that intimacy is organised.

Even more recently, the issue of 'homonormativity' has been raised, whereby a Western (European), middle-class, and largely male worldview dominates sexual minority discourse (Bridges, 2014), and where the "resolution of the 'problem' of homosexuality is found through gradual legal and civil changes resulting in assimilation" (Hicks, 2008, p. 68). Homonormativity creates its own kind of scripted relationships, suggesting that there is a narrow range of expressions of same-sex attractions, behaviours, and intimacy. Homonormativity, for instance, may be said to drive the political movements to marriage, parenting rights, and adoption equality around the world (paralleling acceptable heterosexual norms as a way of fully belonging to a society), and thus scripting acceptable behaviours and relationships in queer communities. As heterosexual partnerships find increasingly diverse intimate expressions, so sexual minority partnerships may find increasingly confined expressions. In this way, some sexual and gender minority identities and expressions may find themselves re-marginalised by people they might consider members of their own communities.

Sexuality

As we noted in Chapter 1, sexuality is a term that relates to the private dimension in which people live out their sexual, intimate, and/or emotional desires (Dunk-West & Hafford-Letchfield, 2011, p. 2). Sexuality is "an intrinsic part of human identity" (Elias & Ryan, 2011, p. 1668). Intimacy and sexuality are frequently conflated in popular discourse because intimacy is a less specific term that may be sexual or non-sexual, and some people remain uncomfortable talking about sex and its sweaty implications. Yet like intimacy, and perhaps more so, sexuality is also highly shaped by its public dimension. A number of authors around the world (Castro Varela, Dhawan, & Engel, 2011; Cocker & Hafford-Letchfield, 2010; Dunk-West & Hafford-Letchfield, 2011; Encarnación, 2011; Oswin, 2010; Schmidt, 2001; Tadele, 2011) have proposed that, like intimacy, the private dimension of sexuality must be understood in public cultural and socio-political contexts, as well as at the individual level. The interplay of these public and private dimensions is reflected in the way sexuality has been treated in the scholarly literature. In that literature, sexuality has usually been understood as focussed on gender and sexual minorities; it is only recently that writers have noted that the emergence of literature about sexual and gender minorities also offers a lens to critique heterosexuality (Tin, 2008/2012). Some authors have portrayed these minoritised sexualities as cultural variants, where the student and practitioner learn something *about* sexual and gender minorities and their needs in order to be more 'culturally competent' in their practice (Mallon, 2008). More recently, this approach has been critiqued by those who claim that such cultural models of education and practice do not take into account the fundamental issue of heteronormativity, and thus do not critique heterosexual values and cultures. Cultural variant approaches have also been criticized for problematising sexual and gender minorities: that is, that sexual and gender minorities have to be explained, while sexual and gender majorities (that is, cisgender heterosexuals) do not because they are normal and natural. Some authors have taken a pragmatic critical approach that comprises both of these perspectives (Cosis Brown & Cocker, 2011): that practitioners and researchers need to understand minoritised sexual identities while at the same time are prepared to critique heteronormativity.

It seems clear that any understanding of sexualities must be able to include understandings of all variations of human sexuality: unfortunately, so far this unified theory of sexuality has proved elusive. Over the years, a great deal of research time and ink has been spilled in attempting to understand the aetiology of homosexuality; any attempt to explain sexual identity that does not also explain heterosexuality is deficient. Nevertheless, these attempts can generally be clustered into three broad categories: essentialism, social constructionism, and life course theory.

Essentialism

An essentialist position posits that individuals are born with a sexual identity, such as hetero- or homosexual. This was the point that Ulrichs and Kertbeny were trying to make. A major developmental task for individuals with nonstandard identities is to discover and claim those essentialised identities. Contemporary essentialist research has focussed on genetic and hormonal 'causes' for sexual and gender identities, and investigates markers such as DNA, brain structure, and even finger length (Rahman & Wilson, 2003). It has been claimed that these markers differ in heterosexuals and homosexuals (we use those terms here deliberately). In the early days of gay and lesbian rights movements, activists have supported such research and conceptualisation because if one is born (or essentially) different, one's difference is not a matter of choice, and therefore any legal or social sanctions against sexual and gender minorities are nothing more than discrimination, thus echoing Ulrichs and Kertbeny. Many, if not most, sexual minority men and women report that they have experienced themselves as different from their peers from their earliest memories (Eliason, 1996; Henrickson et al., 2007; Jay & Young, 1977), which suggests that they believe that their identity is an essential one that has existed at least since birth. Therefore, goes the identity-based argument, sexuality should be treated in the same way as gender, or colour, or race because sexualities are inherent, and therefore no one's 'fault'. Discrimination and stigma may still exist, but in rights-based societies, under an essentialist framework, they can have no basis in law. In the context of our present exploration, then, an essentialist understanding of identity is important because it is a way people made vulnerable by laws have adopted in order to challenge the equity of those laws.

Because we live in heteronormative environments, in general, young people are not exposed to non-heterosexual identities, and therefore non-heterosexual young people must recognise, discover, and reconcile their essential difference through internal processes. This coming out process (Cass, 1979) is one that is familiar to every sexual or gender minority person usually as a lonely search for answers to 'why do I feel different?' and 'where do I belong?' Through exposure to media, and particularly Internet resources, this process is probably quicker and less isolated today than it was even 15 years ago, but it is still a complex time in the life of a queer young person. This process of coming out and recognising one's essential identity is a critical one in the lives of sexual and gender minorities (which can occur at any age), a time in which the individual must reject the heteronormative values and culture that have been instantiated in them. It is a highly individualising time, where the person must choose to value their own experience of identity and truth over that of the dominant social environment in which they live. This learning to value individual experience and truth is the foundation of what we might call a 'queer epistemology'. The individual assesses information they encounter against their individual experience of truth and reality. The individual learns to reject the cultural heteronorms and prioritise their individuality. The challenge then is that they may lose whatever sense of belonging they may have had: at that point, they are truly an island. In some collectivist cultures, particularly Confucian and African cultures where the collective or family is valued more highly than the individual, this process is even more difficult, and can result in a kind of dual identity, where the appearance of the collective identity is maintained, but the individual desire, attraction, behaviour, and experience of identity may be quite different. This is what some cultures mean when they say that 'homosexuality' is a Western import: what is imported, however, is not the sexuality, but the liberal humanist prioritisation of the individual (which we introduced in Chapter 1) over the collective.

What the queer individual will then do is begin to reach out, to construct a new way of belonging through disclosure. A sexual or gender minority individual will learn to reject the vertical identity provided by affiliation with their heteroparents or caregivers and develop more horizontal identities (Solomon, 2012) with like-minded peers. It is no coincidence that a significant way of bonding for many sexual and gender minorities is to share coming out stories, stories of how they experienced themselves as different, stories of oppression, and how they are reconstructing their world. This disclosure of a new identity creates a new way of belonging, and forms a second part of a queer epistemology. A sexual or gender minority who lives in a heteronormative world must disclose in order to be seen for who they 'really' are. The decision to disclose is accompanied by an attempt to engage in authentic intimacy. Here is where the need to belong governs intimacy. Furthermore, the queer person develops what is a kind of bicultural identity, where they must effectively extrapolate themselves into the world in order to fit into it. There is a lovely *New Yorker* cartoon by William Haefli about two apparently gay men standing outside a movie theatre, and one says to the other, "Not another movie about straight people in love. I'm sick of extrapolating" (Figure 3.2).

The individualisation of knowledge validation and the need to disclose in order to belong are experiences that are incomprehensible to most cisgender heterosexual persons because they belong to a world that includes them. This is not the experience of sexual and gender minority persons.

Figure 3.2 "Not another movie about straight people in love. I'm sick of extrapolating."

Source: William Haefeli/The New Yorker Collection/The Cartoon Bank; © Condé Nast

This constant process of individual validation of knowledge and information, and the need to create a new way to belong, form the epistemological foundation of sexual and gender minorities. The difference between heteronormative majorities and sexual and gender minorities, then, is not who they love or who they have sex with: it is how they validate knowledge and information. The knowledge validation values the individual over the collective. It is this difference that contributes to making conversations about sexual identity with heteronormative family members, religionists, and politicians so difficult. The conversations occur in frameworks of non-intersecting epistemologies. It is only in a rights-based framework – which requires an essentialist identity – that political and legal advances can be made.

An essentialist understanding of sexual and gender identity is also crucial to refuting so-called and discredited 'reparative' therapies, which seek to 'repair' the identities of homosexual persons and remake them into heterosexuals (Becksted, 2012). These approaches assume that heterosexuality is normal, and that there is something defective about a non-heterosexual identity. While public behaviours may be reshaped for a time, if we understand that the differences are essential and epistemological, we see that such efforts are futile, unethical, and damaging.

Social constructionism

Social constructionist theories refute notions that sexuality is an inherent condition and proposes that minoritised sexual roles are largely constructed by their social and cultural contexts in order to maintain boundaries around the rest of the community: "The creation of a specialised, despised and punished role of homosexual keeps the bulk of society pure in rather the same way that the similar treatment of some kinds of criminals helps keep the rest of society law-abiding" (McIntosh, 1986, pp. 184–185). The disadvantage of this practice as a means of social control is that some people may become "fixed in their deviance" (p. 184) once they have been so labelled. In a social constructionist approach, labelling people as sexual or gender minorities is, in short, a means of social control. In more contemporary understandings of social constructionism, we find that people construct their public, and to some extent, private, identities in conformity to their social contexts (Foucault, 1978; Greenberg, 1988; Simon & Gagnon, 1973/2009; Wilkerson, Ross, & Brooks, 2009). People learn the sexual stories, the narratives of the intimate (Plummer, 1995) of their cultures; sexual stories are social actions embedded in social words, both symbolic interactions and political processes that render meanings of the self and other (Plummer, 1995, p. 17).

More recent social constructionist approaches to sexuality attempt to reconcile how being gay or lesbian in the social contexts of Los Angeles, London, Stockholm, or Sydney is so different from being a sexual minority in Mumbai, Kampala, Apia, or Seoul. Political and legal environments make a difference, of course, but anyone who has seen movies like *The Wedding Banquet* (Lee, 1993) knows the lengths that sexual minorities must go to in order to appear socially conforming in some cultures. Anthropologists have long noted the existence of homosociality and homosexual behaviour in many cultures, although this lived experience may be quite different from contemporary gay and lesbian identities (Arbodela & Murray, 1985; Blackwood & Wieringa, 1999; Boellstorff, 2005; Brewer, 2005; Chou, 2000; Makofane, 2012; Murray & Roscoe, 1997; Vanita, 2002). Likewise, gender minorities, such as the *hijra* of India, *kathoey* of Thailand (Winter & Udomsak, 2002), *fa'afafine* of Samoa, *(faka)leitis* of Tonga, *lai cai, bong cai, bong lai cai*, and *dong co* of Vietnam (Walters, 2006), *mak nyah* of Malaysia (Equal Rights Trust, 2011), *bissu* of Sulawesi (Graham, 2004), and so forth, are specific to their cultural contexts. Despite these differences, however, socially constructed identities serve a common purpose: they allow sexual and gender majorities to see themselves as majorities, that is, as non-transgressive. If I am a cisgender heterosexual (to use contemporary Western jargon) and I see an extremely effeminate male or very masculine female, a drag performer, someone I identify as transgender, or even someone performing the traditional tasks or taking the sexual positions of the 'other' gender, then I can say with assurance 'I am not like that: I belong to the majority of my culture and community'. Here is the place where the interests of sexual and gender minorities become aligned, particularly around sexual behaviour. In many cultures, for instance, it is perfectly acceptable for men to be the dominant (insertive) partner in sexual activity with another man and still maintain his majoritised identity as heterosexual; however, a man who accepts the so-called submissive (receptive) role – that is, acts (in the eyes of the dominant culture) as if he were a woman – can no longer maintain that majority identity. He has crossed over, and allowed himself to be treated as a woman. The power to identify, to label, and to stigmatise clearly belongs with sexual and gender majorities. Ironically, these majorities need sexual and gender minorities in order to maintain their majority (and therefore power) status, even while their outsider position allows these minorities to critique the majority culture.

All of this is very well in the case of men, the reader may be thinking, but what about women? We know that the sexual identity of women is dynamic: that is, the sexual identities of women are flexible and fluid, particularly when compared to men (Diamond, 2003a, 2003b, 2006; Fingerhut, Peplau, & Ghavami, 2005; Kitzinger & Wilkinson, 1995). Men's sexual identity appears to be stable and 'fixed' quite early in life (Henrickson et al., 2007), but Diamond holds that the prevailing sexual identity models of development have been oversimplified, and based mostly on research with experiences and processes of self-identified ('out') gay men. These simplistic models have been presented to parents and young people, as well as agencies and professions caring for and protecting young people, as the normative pattern for sexual identity development; deviation from this pattern may well cause consternation within these groups. Sexual identities in women appear to be more complex, and are different from what we might call the 'dominant model', in characteristics, process, and outcome (Diamond, 2006, p. 74). Women in opposite-sex marriages who understood themselves as heterosexual may find themselves emotionally attracted to another woman; women in same-sex partnerships may find themselves unexpectedly attracted to men. Not just lesbians, then, or even sexual and gender minority women, but all women have effectively been subject to the dominant narrative of sexual and gender identity development. It seems that even identity development has been dominated by men with the power to define.

The discourse about who is a woman has recently been the subject of heated debates within women's communities. In 2015, a major American women's music festival chose to close rather than to admit transgender women to the festival; a similar Australian festival banned pre-operative transwomen. Activist and academic women have proposed that anyone who has lived even part of their life as male and lived with the privileges conferred on that identity cannot truly identify with the experiences of women (news.com.au, 2015). Transexuality and transgenderism have been labelled as surgical mutilation that maintains male dominance and female subordination (Jeffreys, 1997), and transgender reassignment in children as gender eugenics (Jeffreys, 2012). Other feminist theorists have challenged these notions. It would seem that the need to define and dominate the discourse about sexuality and gender is not entirely limited to men, or even politicians.

Finally, we must acknowledge that in the past several years, some young people have begun to avoid, and even reject, the dominant narrative of sexual and gender identity development. We have begun to hear expressions like 'post-gay' (Russell, Clarke, & Clary, 2009; Savin-Williams, 2005), and young people describe themselves as 'heteroflexible' and 'gender variant', ironically recapitulating the historical and social phylogeny of these identities. Traditional categories such as gay, lesbian, bisexual, and even intersex are less relevant now than they ever have been, and as we saw, alternative, poly-, or non-gendered pronouns are proposed (Chak, 2015). A case could be made that the reality that these options are available signals a victory for women's and gay rights' movements around the world. However, while sexuality and gender are more complicated than ever, these sexual and gender 'variants' are still varieties of something, and that something is the dominant discourse of the cisgender heterosexual. In the context of social constructionist approaches to sexuality and gender, it is the dominance of the heteronormative discourse that marginalises sexual and gender variations.

Life course

Although some authors have suggested that the essentialist and social constructionist perspectives are forever exclusive (DeLamater & Hyde, 1998), in the last few decades, a life course perspective that attempts to integrate these two approaches has emerged. The apparently simple taxonomy of gender and sexuality in fact includes complex factors that comprise biology (DNA), anatomy (the so-called reproductive organs and secondary sexual characteristics), behaviours (who we have sexual activity with), sexual attraction, emotional attraction (who we fall in love with), and fantasies (daydreams and night dreams). As we have seen, in the dominant narratives of sexual and gender identity development, these factors have been used in ways that assume they are aligned with each other, and are static and unchanging throughout our lives. We now know that human identities are significantly more complex, that these factors may not be aligned, they are not static, and that they can and often do evolve and change over the course of a lifetime. The framework for this multidimensional dynamism is reflected in the matrix depicted in Figure 3.1.

The life course perspective of human development (Hammack & Cohler, 2009) combines the essentialist and social constructionist approaches, and proposes that biological desire motivates behaviour, and individuals "internalize the sexual story possibilities" (Hammack, 2005, p. 281) of a culture in order to create lived identities. Individuals not only recognize their essential desires, which probably have an as yet unknown biological basis, but also learn the cultural stories (that is, the socially constructed options) that enable us to construct and express our evolving sexual and gender identities. It is the different cultural stories that make it possible for genders and sexualities to appear so diverse in different cultures. Sexual stories are produced by the meeting of interpersonal lives and social structural patterns. For reasons we can still only hypothesise, the life course trajectories for sexuality, and possibly gender, are different for men and women.

The place where intimacy and sexuality intersect with vulnerability and marginality is now, we hope, clear. It is when others – states, religions, and other power elites – take the power to define who we are (our identities), what we do (our behaviours), and the ways that our identities can be expressed in different cultural contexts that sexual and gender minorities become vulnerable and marginalised communities. The only thing that unifies such astonishingly diverse groups as sexual and gender minorities around the world is their vulnerability to cisgender heterosexuals.

Residential care

Another group of persons who frequently have their sexualities and genders defined, described, and proscribed are persons living in residential care. The abilities of residents to express intimacy and sexuality is both set out and limited not only by the formal rules and regulations of the institution, but the informal values, expectations, and beliefs of the facility staff. Intimacy and sexuality particularly among residents in aged care facilities remains a troubling, misunderstood, and frequently contended issue (Bauer et al., 2013; Gilmer, Meyer, Davidson, & Koziol-McLain, 2010; Shuttleworth et al., 2010), particularly in respect of people living with dementias (Elias & Ryan, 2011; Price, 2012). It is here that residents of institutions – be they aged, disabled, intellectually impaired, persons in state care or custody, or otherwise not empowered to make and express decisions about their intimate, sexual, and gendered life – form common cause with non-institutionalised sexual and gender minorities. Residents are governed by laws, regulations, and even specific protections, but also are at the mercy of staff interpretations of these protections, and personal values of staff.

There is little dispute that sexuality and intimacy contribute to the quality of life of residents in care and their families and carers (Benbow & Beeston, 2012). It could be said that sexuality and intimacy are even more important in the lives of people in residential care because often the only touch residents experience is that of a medical examination or procedure. Residents may be poked, palpated, prodded, and injected, but gentle touch, such as stroking or caressing, may be specifically prohibited as inappropriate. Sexual minorities constitute a significant 'invisible minority' in residential care (Callan, cited in Elias & Ryan, 2011), and their intimacy needs remain largely unknown and unacknowledged. Sexuality in residents with dementia presents a particular challenge because the ethical and legal expectation of consent can be difficult to ascertain (Ehrenfeld et al., 1999; Hajjar & Kamel, 2003). Dementias are not static states, and individuals may move through various states of awareness and competence throughout the day. While the myth of the 'dirty old man' (or woman) behaving inappropriately in the day room has currency, reports of inappropriate sexual behaviour vary between 1.8 and 17.5 percent of residents; this wide variance is attributed to the lack of definition and clarity around this issue (Hayward, Robertson, & Knight, 2012). In fact, inappropriate sexual behaviour is almost invariably subject to staff perceptions about what is inappropriate (Hayward, Robertson, & Knight, 2012). Furthermore, negotiating the sometimes competing interests of residents, staff of various disciplines, families (including partners, children, and grandchildren), and regulatory bodies is complicated, and in the absence of specific guidance, staff are likely to draw on their own values and experiences (Elias & Ryan, 2011).

These issues are consistent internationally. Israeli staff attitudes towards sexual relations in residents with Alzheimer's-related dementia were characterised by confusion and ignorance, and residents were mistreated and humiliated around issues of sexuality (Tabak & Shemesh-Kigli, 2006). American studies have also found negative attitudes in staff towards sexuality in residents, including embarrassment, confusion, and helplessness (Di Napoli, Breland, & Allen, 2013). While staff reactions towards resident expressions of love and care were very positive, reactions to romantic behaviour were more mixed, and included humour and infantilising attitudes ("Isn't that cute"); erotic behaviour aroused strong reactions of anger and resentment (Tabak & Shemesh-Kigli, 2006). Residential care staff responses towards sexual relationships have been described as 'extremely cautionary' (Villar et al., 2014). Residents of care facilities are subject not only to the usual social constructions of sexuality, but also the specific and often *ad hoc* constructions and understandings about sexuality of staff, which may change from day to day, and even shift to shift. Even where policies exist, staff may implement policies according to their own understandings and interpretation of sexuality, or may be heavily influenced by family members. For instance, we are aware that in jurisdictions where sex work has been decriminalised, a number of residential care facilities (including, but not only, aged care facilities) provide residents with access to sex workers, although some staff deeply disapprove of this access. This acknowledgement has been made privately to us; it is certainly not publicised in the brochures because of the risk of public censure – after all, residential facilities are heavily marketed to family members, and the idea of grandma having a sexual relationship with someone other than grandpa is unimaginable. We know of an incident where an older husband and wife entered residential care together, and staff discovered the long-standing mutually consented habit of the husband wearing his wife's undergarments. Care staff were at first shocked, and demanded the practice stop, which caused the couple both great distress; after review by the facility management, their practice was allowed to continue. Undergarments are bits of cloth, imbued with socially constructed meanings, and it is the transgression of these meanings that caused shock to staff, who felt that gender norms were being violated. What purpose would requiring an end to the practice serve? Only the satisfaction of staff cultural norms, and certainly not the wellbeing of the two residents.

We shall explore some of these issues of sexuality in residential care in greater depth in Chapter 6. It is our purpose here to establish that many of the issues about how states and societies manage and control sexuality and intimacy in sexual and gender minorities also apply to how sexuality and intimacy is managed in residential care facilities. Laws, policies, and regulations create vulnerable and marginalised populations and individuals who are not vulnerable or marginalised of themselves.

Note

1 Cisgender is a relative neologism that means a person whose self-identity and self-understanding is consistent with the gender that corresponds to the biological or anatomical gender that was assigned to them at birth; cisgender probably describes most people.

Key questions for Chapter 3

We believe that social work and other human service professionals and researchers need to critique attitudes about intimacy and sexuality, and about sexual and gender minorities. As we saw in the previous chapter, it is the powerful entities and social majorities that create these categories, and put individuals into those categories. We invite you to reflect on your position on some of the key issues raised in this chapter.

- How do you define intimacy? Which aspects of the views we propose do you find challenging?
- How do you define sexuality? Which aspects of the views we propose do you find challenging?
- What language do you use in talking about sexual and gender minorities? How do your understandings shape your language? How does your language shape your understandings?
- Do you find yourself aligning with essentialist, social constructionist, or life course theories of gender and sexuality? Are there other theories of gender and sexuality that you prefer? Why?
- How do you think residential care facilities should manage sexuality in residents? Should different standards apply to individuals who are intellectually compromised? Should intellectually compromised persons be required to conform to socially dominant standards of identity, intimacy, and sexuality? Should they be permitted to be sexual?

4 Critiquing power and privilege

This book assumes that power and privilege exist. In previous chapters, we have suggested that powerful and privileged entities and persons create and manage ideas of vulnerability and marginality by creating and imposing labels of vulnerability and marginality on classes of persons; these are not identities or characteristics that people will normally take on themselves. Once these atomising labels have been applied and these identities established, then powerful elites (powerful because they have the ability to label, and to act as if those labels were real), and indeed entire communities and populations, essentialise these identities. That is, they react to the designated groups as though they were naturally and inherently (and therefore permanently and in every aspect of their lives) vulnerable or marginalised. These labels become self-fulfilling prophesies, as groupings of 'vulnerable' and 'marginalised' persons conceptualise themselves in these ways, and learn to work within a vulnerability or marginalisation framework to achieve their goals, and to access what resources they can by whatever means are available to them. By that point, however, their goals will have become boundaried by the delimitations of vulnerability and marginality, and so may become not only self-fulfilling, but self-perpetuating. Vulnerable people become more vulnerable, and marginalised people become more marginalised. Traditional reflexive-therapeutic social work and other intervention models have been critiqued because they merely assist vulnerable persons to become more comfortable in these delimited frameworks (Payne, 2005). Such critiques challenge much of contemporary Western social work, particularly social work situated in post-Rogerian Western contexts that value client independence, autonomy, competition, and self-determination, and holds 'unconditional positive regard' as the core value of workers for their clients. These critiques challenge social workers in particular to recover their radical (as in 'from the community' grass, bamboo, or flax roots) perspective, and to be aware of often oppressive conditions in which they and their clients are living. In non-Western environments, client independence and autonomy is markedly less valued, and instead, concepts like interdependence, collectivism, familism, cooperation, and social development that is consistent with social cohesion are valorised. This chapter will propose that radical alternatives are necessary not only to assist clients to achieve authentic autonomy and self-determination, but also to achieve a more authentic social cohesion.

Who made your shoes?

The next step in this journey, then, is to critique the nature of power and privilege as ways of creating notions of vulnerability and marginality. Critiquing power and privilege allows us to interrogate it, and not simply accept its labels as received truth. Like most conditions, the nature of privilege is such that it is difficult or impossible to conceptualise outside that privilege, or even to recognise that one is privileged, until one is confronted by the realities and deprivations of a non-privileged life. Privilege is comfortable because it creates access to resources. These resources may be practical, such as clean water and sanitation,[1] food, electricity,[2] or the Internet,[3] or they can include access to less tangible (but no less real) resources such as opportunities, laws, and social protections. The recent literature is replete with efforts to identify privilege and the power that accumulates with privilege, and some social movements have been vociferous in their condemnation of elites who control resources. A 2016 report by Oxfam International, for instance, finds that the richest 62 people in the world control resources equivalent to the combined resources of the planet's poorest 3.6 billion people – 50 percent of the world's population (Oxfam, 2016). Forbes' 2015 list of the world's ten wealthiest people estimates that they had individual assets between US$40.1 billion and US$79.2 billion (Forbes, 2015); to put that in context, if these ten people were countries, all of them individually would be in the top half of the world's nations by GDP. Lest you think that we are only talking about the extraordinarily wealthy, or about other people, can you say who made the shoes you wear? Do you know where they were made? How much the shoemaker was paid to make them? Most of us who can afford books and the time to read them are extraordinarily wealthy compared to most of the world, but we do not often stop to consider this. Our annual incomes may not run into the billions, or millions, but they are probably more than bare subsistence, and most of us who read these words will have access to the essential resources we need to live, the access to these pages (whether bought or borrowed), and the education to read them. We are part of the powerful who influence the world. This is not one of those books that proposes that wealth in and of itself is bad; indeed, some extremely wealthy people use their wealth to create or support charitable causes (e.g., the Bill & Melinda Gates Foundation, or the Buffet Foundation). However, even the most charitable efforts cannot overcome structural inequalities, and the negative outcomes from the unequal global distribution of wealth have dire consequences. The Oxfam report finds that the poorest people on the planet live in areas that are most susceptible to climate change, and are more likely to suffer the effects of climate change. The poorest 50 percent of the world is responsible for only 10 percent of global emissions that create environmental risk (Oxfam, 2016, p. 4), which means that the richest 50 percent are responsible for 90 percent. People in societies with the greatest income inequalities are also more likely to have disparities between genders in health, education, labour market participation, and representation in legislative bodies.

What has created these staggering inequalities? In short, we suggest, it is the way we understand and value wealth. It is the way we have come to value wealth over persons. In the first chapter, we referred to the Deuteronomic attitude that wealth was a sign of divine blessing. Capitalism became the way to obtain that blessing in a more predictable way, and spurred the rise of industry and the economic systems, laws, and policies that favour markets and the accumulation of capital. In the last several decades, industry has had more to do with finance and the development of arcane financial investment instruments (can anyone explain a credit default swap to a lay person?). The world has seen the emergence of a kind of high-priesthood of financiers whose sole purpose is to contrive ways to develop wealth by capitalising on the resources of others, and in the meanwhile, accumulate fantastically large sums of money. (Well, fantastic to those of us who do human service work, anyway.) The development of corporate tax shelters and tax avoidance schemes, intellectual property law (to ensure that the pricing of life-saving pharmaceuticals remains high, for instance), and international trade deals all make sure that the wealthy will continue to get wealthier and the poor will remain poor, and become relatively poorer. We even refer to people now as 'human (or social) capital'. Universities have no longer become merely places of ideas and the building of knowledge: these ideas must be 'monetised'. Business schools rejoice in abundant funding and enrolments, while education, nursing, and human services programmes subsist on slogans like 'We're not in it for the income, but for the outcome'. Academic success is valued by the money researchers attract more than the ideas they produce. It is no longer human beings that are valued, but wealth, and the resources it buys individuals and corporations. Are we indeed more blessed?

The rise of neoliberalism

Neoliberalism is the extension of the free market economic model into government policies and practices, which arose in the 1970s and was popularised by Ronald Reagan in the United States and Margaret Thatcher in the United Kingdom, as well as by governments in Australia and New Zealand (Hewison & Robison, 2006). Although the term is used in various ways by various scholars, the core of neoliberalist approaches include a laissez-faire economic approach (more about this in a moment, as we consider corporations and banks that are 'too big to fail'), small government, the decentralisation of labour relations and weakening of unions, a limited welfare state, and the privatisation of as many traditionally government services as possible, including health, prisons, education, and social services. Neoliberalism differs from classical liberalism in that it relies more on markets and the governments that support them than on popular democracy. Neoliberal governments hold that the private sector is inherently more efficient, and therefore less costly, than the public sector; competition and the motivation for profits are what drive these efficiencies. Lower public costs are desirable because they allow for a reduced tax burden for the wealthy, who (the theory presumes) will then reinvest it as capital.[4]

Loïc Wacquant has dubbed the neoliberal state "neo-Darwinist" (Wacquant, 2004/2009, p. 5) because it "erects *competition* and celebrates unrestrained individual responsibility – whose counterpart is collective and thus political irresponsibility" (emphasis in original). Yet it seems even the free market is not so free, and certainly not free to the public: ProPublica lists 956 private companies in the US alone who have been recipients of US$618 billion in government (that is, taxpayer) bailout money (ProPublica, 2016). These recipients are in the state-owned enterprise (mortgage lender), insurance, auto, banking, finance, investment funds, and mortgage services sectors. Forbes also reported that the US Federal Reserve lent US$16 *trillion* to non-US corporations and banks (Greenstein, 2011). To be fair, the US government has netted a total of roughly US$65 billion so far (in repayments and other revenues) from the US corporate bailouts, but such bailouts are hardly examples of laissez-faire market economics.

Hewison and Robison (2006) have suggested that neoliberal policies have not caught on in Asia in the same ways as in Western economies with longer traditions of market economies, despite the Asian financial crisis of the first decade of the 21st century. They suggest that Asian resistance to neoliberalism is found not in vested market interests, but in older, entrenched powerful elites. In Europe, since 2008, bailout funds combining IMF, World Bank, and other funds totalling over €544 billion were delivered to individual governments that are part of the European Stability Mechanism, although many of these loans were necessitated by these governments lending to private sector financial institutions. The usual argument given by lenders and lending apologists is that these various corporate entities were 'too big to fail', and that may well be true because of the potential calamity that would be visited upon communities, local governments, employees, individual investors, retirees, and so forth, but the illusion of a free market has been well unmasked.

Yet when neoliberal governments plan for the delivery of other services to individual tax-payers, citizens, and residents, there is certainly another text that is preached. Individual recipients of legitimate government resources and services are demonised: Wacquant, whose primary interest is in criminology, writes that government

> then withdraws into its regalia functions of law enforcement . . . and its symbolic mission of reasserting common values through the public, anathematization of deviant categories – chief among them the unemployed 'street thug', and the 'pedophile,' viewed as the walking incarnations of the abject failure to live up to the abstemious ethic of wage work and sexual self-control.
>
> (pp. 5–6)

It would seem that the liberal humanism that created the rise of individualism has evolved into *neoliberal* humanism, and the sacred essence, once located in persons, has been relocated from the individual to the corporate. This evolution has been confirmed in the US by Supreme Court rulings (Citizens United *v.* FEC in 2010 and Burwell *v.* Hobby Lobby, 2014), which declared that corporations have the same legal rights as individual persons (Park, 2014). Along the way, the rights of individuals have been increasingly subject to control by neoliberal governments.

In a neoliberal economic environment, on the one hand, governments attempt to withdraw themselves from the provision of welfare services to vulnerable and marginalised persons, and on the other hand, they set themselves up, through technocrats, as enforcers of public good, insisting on particular kinds of behaviours (workfare programmes, child-rearing subsidies) that are consistent with dominant class and cultural values. Wacquant notes that neoliberal governments have three tools at their disposal to deal with undesirable, offensive, or threatening persons: socialising (e.g., rehousing homeless persons, requiring that individuals undertake work or education); medicalising (e.g., classifying persons with non-conforming behaviours as having a health or mental health disorder, and requiring them to be treated); or penalizing (e.g., through forced incarceration). All of these options, and incarceration in particular, make the problems of deviance disappear to the general public and electorate. It is not surprising to hear many politicians taking a tough stance on crime because in doing so, they signal their participation in dominant community values, and implicitly promise an increased sense of security to the electorate. It will be noted, however, that in its role as enforcer of the public good through insisting on particular kinds of behaviours, neoliberal governments create classes of marginalised persons, and either socialise, medicalise, or incarcerate them. Undesirability and offensiveness are cultural constructions: what may be undesirable, or offensive, in one cultural context may be the norm in another cultural context or generation. Yet governments are elected, and the electorate wants to feel secure (which is separate from actually *being* secure), and so governments are encouraged by the electorate to enforce conformity. We have heard the well-known truism that incarcerated persons are usually people of colour (in White-dominant societies): in the US as early as 1990, 40 percent of African American males ages 18–35 were in prison, on probation, or parole; in Washington D.C., the proportion was 42 percent, and in Baltimore, the number was over 56 percent (Wacquant, 2004/2009). In 2014, African Americans were 40 percent of America's prison population, although they made up only 12 percent of the total population (Tonn, 2014). This trend is mirrored elsewhere: in Aotearoa New Zealand, indigenous Māori women made up 58 percent of the women's prison population and Māori men were 51 percent of the men's, despite the fact that Māori are only about 15 percent of the total population; Pacific Islanders make up 7 percent of the population but 12 percent of the prison population; Europeans (Whites) make up about 69 percent of the population, but only 33 percent of the prison population (Statistics New Zealand, n.d.). In Australia, although Aboriginal and Torres Strait Islanders make up 3 percent of the population, they are 28 percent of the prison population (Tonn, 2014).

In short, power, and the privilege to name, contain, and control vulnerable and marginalised people and groups, have increasingly been assumed by the state, and in the West, by markets and the states that support them. The notion of individual autonomy, independence, and self-determination is illusory. It is essential that the human service practitioner, researcher, and policymaker be aware of the increasing concentration of power in these elites, and to be aware that their clients, research participants, or beneficiaries are largely artefacts of the powerful elites who created them. In the same way that male erectile dysfunction was not a public issue until there was a pill to cure it, people are made vulnerable or marginalised by markets and governments that have a purpose in doing so. That purpose is the increase of private wealth and the increasing restriction of social welfare.

Education may not be the answer

One of the core tenets of radical theory is that if people are made aware of their oppression, or conscientised, they will rise up to resist it (Freire, 1970). Education would then seem to be a way of conscientising people. However, just as power and privilege exist in practice, policy, and research, it is also reproduced even by well-meaning educators. The issue of privileging elites through the colonial concepts of race and indigeneity are well documented (Bennett, 2015; Ford & Kelly, 2005; Hastie & Rimmington, 2014; Shin, 2015; Todd, McConnell, & Suffrin, 2014; Wang, 2004; Zufferey, 2013). This is the process whereby usually White colonial powers enforced their authority and economic advantage onto darker-skinned natives. Even where attempts are made in the present day to incorporate minoritised and indigenous epistemologies into classroom environments and discussions, often these perspectives are presented as cultural artefacts, and rather than disrupting networks of power, they 'dumb down' minority epistemologies (Quinlivan et al., 2014) so that they become almost cartoonish. Attempts at colour blindness "can actually function to obscure and perpetuate racial inequalities and racist oppression" (Matthews, 2011, p. 9). The literature on the privileges of male gender, of course, is rich and transdisciplinary (Kaufmann & Wamsted, 2015; Semali & Shakespeare, 2014), and the issue of privilege by sexuality (Case, Hensley, & Anderson, 2014; Geiger & Jordan, 2014) and cisgender (Johnson, 2013) was addressed in the previous chapter. Recently, the issue of privileging sexuality over asexuality has appeared (Emens, 2014). To add complexity, privilege and power can be intersectional, where a privileged identity, such as being White or male, co-exist with an unprivileged identity, such as being a sexual or gender minority (Parent, DeBlaere, & Moradi, 2013).

Knowles et al. (2014) have challenged the notion that racially dominant groups have the luxury of rarely noticing their race or the privileges racial dominance confers. They have suggested that racially dominant groups – specifically Whites in America – manage their identities to dispel the possibilities that their accomplishments were not fully earned and to disassociate themselves from a group that has benefitted from unfair social advantages. There are three possible strategies that Whites use: to deny the existence of privilege, to distance themselves from the privileged status, or to dismantle systems of privilege and power, beginning with disavowing their own privileges. Of these, Knowles et al. suggest that dismantling White systems of privilege as a strategy of White identity management is preferred. This analysis and strategy can readily be extended to any nation and privileged identity. During debates over same-sex marriage, for instance, the actress Charlize Theron disavowed her privilege as a member of an opposite sex couple, and promised that she and her male partner would not marry until their same-sex friends could do so (Huffpost Entertainment, 2011). While such stances may be trivialised as tokenistic, in fact, for public figures to disavow their privilege sends clear signals to people who otherwise might not stop to consider how privileged they are.

In addition to the identity attributes, dominant Western epistemologies and language are also privileged in practice and education. English, in one form or another, is the dominant international language of meetings and scientific publications, and concepts and values that are not easily expressed in English are modified so that they can be expressed. Although 10 years ago, English was the language of over 70 percent of websites (Paolillo, 2005), that proportion shrunk to less than 54 percent by early 2016 (W3Techs, 2016), suggesting that English – while still very dominant on the Internet – is losing its near-exclusive status. Furthermore, even in this postmodern era with the increasing availability of qualitative and mixed method research methodologies and high quality journals and publications, positivist epistemologies with their notions of 'science' that are heavily quantitative dominate the literature of helping, and are certainly privileged by many disciplines and funders. Quantitative research in English that is done by White, cisgendered heterosexuals largely remains the standard against which other publications are assessed.

Even thoughtful and critically aware educators, researchers, and practitioners, it seems, are bounded by the complex and thorny realities of the oppressive contexts that we have inherited and in which we function. If educators, researchers, and practitioners, whose role it is to be aware of these issues, are confronted by these issues at every turn, how can we possibly expect politicians and bureaucrats to manage them?

Is there any hope?

In the short term, we as human service providers cannot escape the privileged frameworks we have inherited, although we must do all we can not to perpetuate privilege, and to challenge notions of wealth as the object of our longing and signifier of our success. By being aware of these frameworks and the effects they have on teaching, research, and helping relationships, particularly with people who are labelled vulnerable and marginalised, we can critique them and mitigate their power. On a macro scale, one way forward is to question whether measures of national wealth such as the gross domestic product (GDP) are the best ways to assess the social health of a nation. Less familiar indices such as the Gini coefficient measure the income distribution and inequalities within a country. The Gini coefficient has also been used to assess other areas of social development, such as education, opportunity, and income. Although the Gini coefficient is also flawed, it is a step towards developing measures of the social health of nations that move beyond wealth as the primary indicator of a nation's social health. Other measures exist. Bhutan, for instance, has pioneered a 'Gross National Happiness Index' (Centre for Bhutan Studies & GNH Research, 2015), and doubtless other measures will emerge as the accumulation of wealth and capital are challenged as the dominant measures of a nation's wellbeing.

Another way forward on a more micro level is to use alternative approaches to practice and research. Professionalisation in the social services has been critiqued, especially by some indigenous groups, as the way 'expert' practitioners and researchers come into communities with answers to questions the communities did not know they had. Researchers who approach communities with a paternalistic 'I'm a researcher and I'm here to tell you what's wrong with you' attitude have engendered suspicion in minoritised communities labelled as vulnerable and marginalised for decades. It is little surprise that such communities do not readily welcome outside researchers. One of us had occasion to provide consultation work on how a Pacific Island nation was managing their response to HIV. People from many sectors were interviewed. When the time came for the exit presentation, the suspicion in the room was palpable because this was a group of people who had been told by many expert consultants how much they were doing wrong. This time, the presentation focussed on what was going well, and allowed the community to identify their own priorities for development. The attitude in the room changed from resigned and defensive to hopeful. Contemporary research methodologies, such as participatory action research where the researcher enters into a close alliance with the community, encourages them to develop relevant research questions and methodologies, and encourages community members to participate in researching problems and solutions, are far more likely to be welcome and successful. Inclusive research methodologies will be explored further in Chapter 7.

One of the challenges of contemporary social work is that it has inherited an array of 'expert' practice models, particularly from psychodynamically rooted theoretical approaches. 'Clients' with 'problems' have been taught to seek 'expert' advice, and social workers have been instructed by neoliberal agencies to provide help in the most risk-averse way possible. A key component of contemporary social work pedagogy is to teach students that they are not experts in solving clients' problems, but instead should empower and resource clients to address and resolve their own challenges. Furthermore, many people called social workers throughout the world are employed by statutory governmental agencies to administer government programmes and policies: they have authority to require compliance from clients under threat of withholding resources, or of punitive action, including removing children and recommending arrest for serious noncompliance. Whether such statutory work can be considered expert, or even social work, is beyond the scope of the present discussion, but such work is clearly imbued with power and control.

The challenge to all helping professions is to carefully consider their philosophical frameworks, epistemologies, and ethical underpinnings in order to avoid replicating and reproducing power and privilege – whether the privilege of expert, or the power of the state. The increasing internationalisation of social work and the space that has at last been created to hear indigenous and aboriginal voices has allowed time for reflection on how social work in particular is theorised, practiced, and researched. Contemporary social work has the opportunity to extend itself beyond its historical top-down heuristic to what Payne calls a 'modern' model (Payne, 2005), where theory, agency, worker, and client are co-creators in the development of understandings of theory and practice. This heuristic is not static, but dynamic, and informed by the social, political, economic, and intellectual environments from which they emerge (Noble & Henrickson, 2014, p. 7). At the micro level, the practitioner and client enter into an iterative, dialogic relationship where practitioner or researcher her/himself sets aside expert privilege and becomes a more or less equal partner in the conversation. This is not easy, of course, because only those with privilege can set it aside, and certainly clients will continue to perceive workers as more powerful than the workers perceive themselves because the worker has access to resources that the client wants or needs. The worker cannot pretend that the cage of privilege (like the cages of ethnicity, race, gender, or power) is not there, nor can they realistically expect to step in and out of that cage at will. Nevertheless, an iterative, dialogic, hermeneutic process that gradually moves towards authentic truth, insight, and liberation is a way of empowering the client, and encouraging them to move beyond their self-limitations as vulnerable or marginalised. To work in this kind of authentic way, however, requires both significant reflexivity and self-awareness, and risk both by the worker and client. It requires a critical engagement with the epistemological frameworks that professional social work has inherited. But this critical engagement, with all its self-awareness of power and privilege, is a way forward that will challenge neoliberal notions of power, privilege, and labelling, and manualised compliance with a state agenda. This kind of engagement may serve as an exemplar to other disciplines that will help them to challenge received notions of vulnerable and marginalised clients. This kind of engagement may help individuals, groups, and societies into more authentic understandings of self and of social cohesion.

Notes

1 UN Water reports that 783 million people globally do not have access to clean water, and 85 percent do not have access to adequate sanitation (UN Water, 2013); the report notes that wealthier nations are extending their footprint over poorer nations to gain greater access to scarce resources such as water.

2 The World Bank estimates that access to electricity is as low as 5.1 percent in South Sudan, 6.4 percent in Chad, 6.5 percent in Burundi, 9.5 percent in Liberia, and 9.8 percent in Malawi, among the nations in Africa that fall below the 10 percent mark (World Bank, 2015). Other nations that fall below an arbitrary 50 percent access include Afghanistan, Angola, Benin, Burkina Faso, Cambodia, Central African Republic, Republic of the Congo, Eritrea, Ethiopia, The Gambia, Kenya, Democratic Republic of Korea, Lesotho, Madagascar, Mali, Mozambique, Namibia, Niger, Papua New Guinea, Rwanda, Sierra Leone, Somalia, Sudan, Swaziland, Tanzania, Togo, Tuvalu, Uganda, Vanuatu, Yemen, Zambia, and Zimbabwe.

3 A September 2015 report on global broadband finds that 57 percent (four billion people) of the global population still do not or cannot access the Internet regularly; in developing nations, 25 percent fewer women than men have access, and 90 percent of the world's poorest countries do not have access to the Internet (Broadband Commission for Digital Development, 2015). It would seem many of them do not have electricity anyway.

4 The reality seems to be somewhat different; see Dolan (2014), who challenges the myth of the reinvestment of wealth.

Key questions for Chapter 4

This chapter has suggested that vulnerability and marginality have become essentialised categories, and that these categories have been produced and enforced by neoliberal states and market economies in order to increase private wealth and restrict social welfare. Human service practitioners, researchers, and policymakers must be aware that their clients, research participants, or beneficiaries are largely artefacts of the powerful entities that created them, and are made vulnerable or marginalised by markets and governments.

- In your view, should large financial institutions and companies be allowed to fail, or should governments always be a financier of last resort to ensure that such large employers and tax-paying entities cannot fail?
- What are some alternatives to GDP to measure the health and wellbeing of nations?
- In what ways are you privileged? In what ways do you have power? In what ways are you prevented from having privilege? In what ways are you disempowered?
- Is there any issue about which you feel strongly enough that you would be willing to forgo the privileges you have?
- Who made your shoes?

5 Delivery of care
Setting out the challenges

Up until now, our discussions have been mostly theoretical, although they have been grounded in our practice experience. In the second section of this book, we will consider more practice-oriented applications of these ideas. We begin in this chapter with some of the challenges that occur when delivering care to so-called vulnerable and marginalised groups.

We have suggested in previous chapters that vulnerability and marginality are categories that are established by elites in policy and legislation in order to manage people with less power or privilege. These categories are then replicated from the top down throughout the human services sectors in health, mental health, social work and social services, disability, and criminal justice. Such categorisation is defended by policymakers who say they are attempting to provide services and support with the greatest efficiency and the lowest risk to the maximum number of people at the lowest cost to the taxpayer. The demand for increasing efficiencies, however, generally comes about as neoliberal legislatures allocate funds to stimulate enterprise and reduce the burden from taxes on the corporate sector. Already under-resourced sectors such as social welfare, health, and education are then required by public funders, mandated by legislatures, to support increasing numbers of people with flat or decreasing resources. These decreasing resources are the result of legislative choices. Because of these state priorities, increasing demands of accountability are placed on the human services sectors, including not only agencies, but also managers, workers, and clients. This top-down service delivery model – the so-called 'catalytic' model (Payne, 2005) – is then reproduced throughout these sectors; for instance, a physician remains in charge of a patient's care, whether in the community, in a mental health facility, or in residential aged care. While maintaining the appearance of fairness and economic accountability, the modern neoliberal state effectively replicates the three groups codified by the Elizabethan Poor Law in 1601. The 'Old Poor Law' (as it eventually became known) was foremost designed to maintain public order (as were all the Tudor poor laws and their antecedents) rather than out of a sense of compassion for the poor. Paralleling the 1601 law, the first of these contemporary groupings (in contemporary terms) is the 'worthy'; that is, people who have provided (through work), or who are likely to provide (such as the very young), some yield for public investment; these are people who are temporarily out of work, but who are willing to work. The second group is 'less worthy' people; that is, people who are unlikely to provide much yield for investment (such as the very old or the severely disabled), but are unlikely to be productive through no 'fault' of their own. The third group is the 'least worthy' or the 'bad': the criminal, deviant, or lazy person. The state provides the minimum amount of services necessary to manage the needs of people in these various groups: it provides more investment in the worthy groups, and less investment in the less worthy.[1] State investment in the least worthy group is usually limited to 'protecting the public' from 'bad people' such as criminals.

Social bonds and social control

Neoliberal governments expect that private for-profit and charitable sectors, private individual and corporate investors, or individuals (such as unpaid family caregivers) will fill the gaps in public resources with their money or time. The contemporary and controversial trend to develop 'social bonds' or 'social impact bonds' for services traditionally provided by the state such as staffing prisons, delivering mental health care, or child protection is an example of this cost and risk-shifting to private investors (Cahalane, 2014; Jeram & Wilkinson, 2015). (This cost shifting echoes the compulsory collections taken up in English churches to support the parish indigent under the Poor Rate of 1547.) Holders of social bonds, private investors, are paid a dividend by governments when agreed outcomes are achieved. With social bonds, governments incentivise private investors to require that service providers meet agreed targets in order for the investor to harvest from government the profit from their investment. The dividend, of course, is paid with taxpayer money, so the net financial benefit to the public is as yet unclear. Nevertheless, the shifting of risk from the public to the private sector is understood by advocates as a benefit. Social bonds are controversial because investors are financial, and are motivated by profit, rather than by compassion, altruism, or professional responsibility. Investors usually have no experiences in social services delivery, and therefore may not understand that a successful outcome for a client may be using the toilet every day instead of soiling the bed, or not assaulting another resident, or not attempting to harm themselves. The so-called 'success metric' of these bonds is unclear (Savedoff & Madan, 2015), and evaluation models that have been proposed to date are not sufficiently robust (Fiennes, 2013), so that social bonds remain an unproven strategy. Social bonds are also controversial because they are seen by critics to use the least powerful people in society as objects, off the back of whom the wealthy and privileged stand to gain even more wealth. Investors may bring pressure to bear on agencies and workers to produce measureable outcomes that may or may not be related to the benefit of the child, client, resident, patient, or inmate. Social bonds are perceived by critics as a way for governments to privatise essential services that are rightly the function of public welfare; privatised structures may incentivise unethical agencies to cover up problems such as abuse or underperformance (Press, 2015). It is both suggestive and encouraging to see that in August 2016, the US Justice Department made the decision to phase out its use of private prisons, citing 'safety concerns' (BBC News, 2016b).

As we have seen, public resources are provided at the cost of increased social control, after the manner of Bentham's panopticon (a building whose inmates must assume they are under observation at all times), with increasing control of the less worthy ("Time for your shower!") and the most control of the least worthy ("Sixty minutes exercise in the yard begins now, then back to your cell!"). Drug testing beneficiaries is another method of maintaining social control – one that appears to have failed mightily. In the US, vast sums of money are being spent on drug testing welfare recipients, to little effect: in Florida, only 2.6 percent of welfare recipients tested positive for any substance, compared with 8 percent of the general population, and in Michigan, no substance misusers were identified (Cunha, 2014). In New Zealand, out of 8,001 beneficiaries tested, only 22 (0.27 percent) tested positive for substances or refused to be tested (Savage, 2014). In every case in the US, costs of testing outweighed any possible savings identified by excluding substance misusing beneficiaries. Social control maintains vulnerability and reinforces marginality: it is difficult to feel empowered when you are required to look for work in order to receive a public benefit or required to urinate in a bottle, when you are chronically unwell, or when you are in prison.

However, there are additional consequences to this kind of categorisation. The prevailing paradigm of assessment/diagnosis and care for vulnerable and marginalised people is problem-oriented and deficit-focussed.

The care manager must focus on multiple 'stakeholders', not just on caring for one individual. There are regulations, compliance and audit costs, and funding for the long-term survival of the agency, as well as staffing and other resource concerns. It is small wonder, then, that in a contracting funding environment that prioritises business over caregiving decisions, the care manager, who may have entered their profession with high ideals, must learn to make decisions not only about how to maximise increasingly scarce resources, but how to minimise the risk presented to the organisation (and the public) by the client or service user. This problem-oriented approach inevitably leads to a risk-management perspective (based on problems and deficits) rather than a salutogenic (Greene & Cohen, 2005) or wellbeing-focussed perspective based on the strengths, resilience, and the needs of the individual, even for the best-intentioned carer. Care is managed and rationed for the convenience of the institution, not the resident, client, or patient. The individual (or their family) exchanges autonomy and privacy for services. We will consider the possibilities and advantages of wellbeing-focussed approaches in the next chapter. In this chapter, we will explore some of the risks and consequences to risk-management and deficit-focussed perspectives.

A risk-management perspective results in clients, patients, and residents being problematised by practitioners, staff, and management. Managers and governance bodies understandably (from their perspectives) want to minimise risk to an organisation, and so create policies and protocols that minimise institutional risk, and require consistent and authorised approaches to risky situations. Such approaches prohibit or negatively value creativity and untried or unapproved interventions. This means that the same things that are seen to minimise risk to an organisation will be done over and again, regardless of whether they improve the lives of clients or service users, or indeed limit the risk to the organisation. This top-down approach creates a dilemma for care workers. Care workers – nurses, social workers, occupational and recreational therapists, support workers, and the range of care workers – are very likely to have chosen their professions for the most altruistic of reasons, and with the best of intentions. But in an institutional context with limited resources, when clients 'act out' or 'misbehave', or are demanding, fractious, or just unpleasant, it is easy to label these clients as difficult, or non-compliant. The altruism of professionals transforms from selfless concern for the wellbeing of others to managing those others to conform to the institutionally expected standards of behaviour. Such labelling may be compelled by risk-management protocols. Protocols are cited, and client behaviour is problematised and contained. Yet is it not the under-resourced institutions and systems in which care workers must function that are the problem, not the client? Decisions made by over-worked staff are reduced to essential care and the management of risk. Client or resident wellbeing is a secondary consideration. We will examine this idea below by considering a couple of particular groups of persons.

Equity and fairness

A moment ago, we made passing reference to fairness, and before we continue, a short consideration of fairness and equity is in order. Although these are philosophical concepts with lengthy histories and applications beyond the scope of this chapter, we may say that fairness is a complex, culturally constructed concept having to do with access to resources (Schäfer, Haun, & Tomasello, 2015). Equity is generally understood as the quality of fairness, both in Hobbes' sense of reason (Sorell, 2016) and as a set of values that guide policy and resource allocation. Equity in health policy, for instance, establishes a set of desirable health outcomes for a given population, and ensures that the resources necessary to achieve those outcomes are provided. Fairness is often constructed as making equal resources available to classes of persons who generally share the same characteristics. People with greater needs require more resources than those to which they usually have access, and people with fewer needs require access to fewer resources. People who contribute more to a project should receive more benefits from the project than those who contributed less. People who save for their retirement, or who work and pay taxes into a public retirement scheme, should be better off than those who do not save. These apparently commonsense approaches to fairness would seem to apply regardless of whether the contribution is in labour, investment of money or other resources, or paying taxes, and the benefits are a share of the harvest, dividends, or public benefits. A recent study found, for instance, that in a Western developed nation context, children distributed 'profits' from a communal exercise in exact proportion to the amount that each person contributed (Schäfer, Haun, & Tomasello, 2015). However, in the same study, in an egalitarian African pastoralist community, the amount that a person contributed to the enterprise was not considered at all as children made decisions about allocating profits. In other words, in a developed Western context, those who had the ability to contribute also reaped the benefits, while in the pastoralist group, benefits were shared out equally regardless of contribution. The difference in African concepts of fairness were also demonstrated in the very real-world challenge of rationing limited antiretroviral medications to people living with HIV in Lesotho (Armstrong, 2010). While an algorithm for eligibility for medications and patient selection was devised by the World Health Organisation, in practice, the WHO algorithm was abandoned by clinicians in favour of a first come-first served approach (even though the clinicians' approach would seem to reward those who had sufficient health and were able to mobilise resources to attend the medication clinic). Which of these is fairer? Which approaches ensured equity? It depends on who you are, and where you are.

The challenges of assessing and constructing equity, fairness, and need are easily illustrated by a classroom exercise. Students are all seated in traditional rows and files, and a wastepaper bin is placed at the front and centre of the classroom. Each student must remain in their place, and is given one wadded up sheet of paper. Students are then told that they must remain in place, and that anyone who can toss their paper into the bin will be provided with special privileges for the day. Clearly, students in the front of the room will have an advantage over those in the back, and students in the centre will be advantaged over students seated on the sides. Even though all students have been provided with exactly the same resources and the goal is exactly the same for all students (it is equitable), the situation is not fair: students in the back and sides of the room are disadvantaged, and in order to attain the goal, will probably require additional resources (such as more sheets of paper in order to make more tries on the bin) or special arrangements (such as changing the rules to allow them to move, or even moving the bin). We must then amend our concept of what is equitable – making equal resources available to all classes of persons to achieve the same outcome – to the issue of fairness: what will allow all students an equal opportunity to toss their paper in the bin. All students then could take advantage of whatever resources or arrangements they needed to achieve their goals. We might say that a student-centred approach, taking into account location, resources, and abilities, will be necessary for all students to achieve the goal. Sometimes, it seems, in order to be fair, we may need to reconsider what we mean by equitable.

Managerial risk management

In the mid-1980s – the early days of the HIV epidemic on the East Coast of the US – in urban areas, HIV was most prevalent in communities of injection drug users. One of the great frustrations of medical care providers – most of whom were well-educated middle-class Whites – was the seeming intransigence of injection drug users – most of whom were people of colour and largely poor – as they circulated through emergency departments and temporary stays as hospital patients in medical crises. One physician (we will call him Tom) in particular remains in the memory of one of the authors. Tom expressed profound frustration at the non-compliance of one of his hospital patients (we will call him Howard) with a very long history of street drug use. Howard, a Black man, had been admitted through the emergency department in an acute medical crisis because of his HIV. Once he was admitted, Howard was rude to staff, refused medication, would not eat hospital food, and would not accept the batteries of tests that were required to establish exactly what was wrong with him this time. The best efforts of Tom, a well-educated and respected White physician, were being thwarted by Howard, a poorly educated and belligerent street drug user. In frustration, Tom ordered restraints on the patient, which (perhaps not surprisingly) only made Howard's verbal abuse of staff worse, and increased Howard's resistance to procedures.

What Tom had not considered (or had not had time to consider) was that on the street, Howard was extremely successful. For many years, Howard had found enough money to purchase his illicit drugs and was able to secure the equipment to inject the drugs (at a time when even possessing this equipment was illegal). He chose when and where to inject himself. In the midst of these activities, he found sufficient food, and negotiated his way through the complex social structures of the street drug scene, using his own language and vocabulary, finding food that was sufficiently appealing to him and shelter that he chose. Howard was well-known and respected on the streets for his street-savvy and his ability to survive. He was autonomous and largely self-sufficient. Once infected with HIV, however, in those pre-AZT days, Howard was at the mercy of the medical and social care environment. After he was admitted to the hospital, he was managed by people who did not speak his language, and expected him to understand theirs. He was put in an environment where every aspect of his life was controlled by strangers. Needles were inserted into his body with or without his cooperation. He was provided with pills or potions that he was expected to take without question. He was served hospital food by aides who were afraid to enter his room. His social supports were very limited. He was stripped of his autonomy. And when he rebelled in an attempt to regain some control over his own body, he was deemed 'dangerous' or non-compliant, and physically restrained on the orders of a White man. It is little wonder that this clash of cultures and its historical resonance resulted in misunderstanding and frustration for everyone. Yet the hospital staff – the people who had the power – were responsible for the medical management of Howard, for their own safety, and that of other patients. They followed hospital protocol, identified, labelled, and recorded forever his behaviour as risky and dangerous, and responded with increasingly restrictive measures. At this remove, I do not remember if Howard was given sedation to make him more compliant, or at least less resistant, but that would not surprise me. No one 'won' this difficult encounter. While there is no glory in using street drugs, had hospital staff demonstrated some respect for Howard's autonomy and his ability to survive for many years in environments where they would be unlikely to survive even for a few hours, his hospital stay might have been a little easier for everyone. This was the early days of HIV, however, and it is quite likely that staff wanted as little to do with Howard as possible, and turned their attentions towards patients who would be more appreciative of their efforts.

Let us highlight this point: no one did anything wrong in Howard's case. Staff were simply following an approved protocol designed to minimise risk to vulnerable patients and to ensure that staff were also not put at risk. Other ways of getting alongside Howard, of hearing his story and his concerns, respecting his autonomy, and his anger at losing it, would probably have taken more valuable staff time, even if they were willing to do these things, or had management approved such approaches. But Howard was only an injection drug user who worked the streets, and hardly worth the extra time to work with him in a different way.

In April 2015, global media reported the case of a 78-year-old Iowa state legislator, Henry Rayhons, who was charged with felony sexual abuse because he had sex with his wife, Donna, eight days after he had been told by staff at the residential aged care facility (RACF) where she lived that that they believed she was mentally unable to agree to sex (Belluck, 2015). Donna was in an RACF because she had been diagnosed with severe dementia, and had been judged by staff, including her physician, to be incapable of consenting to sex. Both Henry and Donna were widowed, and had married each other in 2007. According to press accounts, staff acknowledged that Donna was always pleased to see her husband, but Donna's daughter by her first marriage was concerned about inappropriate sexual contact, and this prompted staff to raise these concerns with Henry. Following an incident where Henry reportedly had sexual relations with Donna (he contested this, according to press accounts), her daughter petitioned for guardianship of her mother, and restricted Henry's visits. Henry was arrested soon after Donna died. At a jury trial, Henry was found not guilty. At great personal and financial cost to everyone involved, this case highlighted issues of staff management of a person living with dementia, the ability of a person living with dementia to consent to sex (Leys & Rodgers, 2015), and the rights of the individual. Again, in this instance, staff were following protocols that had been established, yet the situation disintegrated into a public spectacle, which was surely painful for everyone.

Dementias are cruel conditions, of course, as family members and friends watch the person they knew gradually fade away. Dementias are also not predictable. At what point does a person living with a dementia lose her autonomy and the right to make decisions about what happens to her own body? Residents of most care facilities are rarely touched except for medical procedures and personal hygiene. Can any of us imagine a life without loving or compassionate touch? Yet staff of the Iowa facility were following protocols and orders established to minimise risks to a 'vulnerable' resident, and minimising risks to themselves (although, this time, the risks were more likely legal than the physical risk presented by the 78-year-old Howard). Except that protocols, which are clear, are not designed for situations that are not clear. Unclear situations must be reconstructed to fit the protocols. It is hardly surprising, then, that staff made a conservative recommendation to minimise what they perceived as risk to all the individuals and the institution in this difficult situation.

Howard and Henry are only two examples of situations found around the world. We read about people living with mental illness in West Africa who are kept in chains because their relatives do not know what else to do with them (Adjovi, 2016); treatment for mental health conditions is unknown or unavailable. We know at least anecdotally of cases where residents of care facilities are kept highly sedated in order reduce their demand on staff time. We hear of staff frustrations at too many demands and not enough resources, or when residents or patients act out on their powerlessness or boredom, or their lack of autonomy or of a future, and the only staff resource is increasing restriction or control, either physical or pharmaceutical, of these residents. Social control becomes even more obvious when persons living with mental health disorders are detained in police cells (BBC News, 2016a; Tait, 2015) because there are no other resources available to manage them. All of these methods are ways of managing risk because alternative resources are overstretched or simply not available. These situations are neither fair nor equitable. It hardly seems likely that social bonds, designed to improve accountability, are likely to be adequate responses to lacunae in a sector.

Intimacy in residential care

There is a clear consensus in the international literature that sexuality is an intrinsic part of human identity (Elias & Ryan, 2011), and that intimacy and sexuality in aged care in particular is a troubling, misunderstood, and frequently contended issue (Bauer, Fetherstonhaugh, et al., 2013; Shuttle-worth et al., 2010). There is also strong support in the literature that there is no age limit on sexual responsiveness, or on the need for intimacy (Ben-bow & Beeston, 2012). Sexuality and intimacy contribute to the quality of life of aged persons in care (Hillman, 2008). Understandings of sexu-ality have also changed over the generations, as the opportunities for all kinds of sexual and intimate relationships have increased. In a number of countries, marriage equality has been written into law. Sexual and gender minorities constitute a significant invisible minority in aged care research (Callan, in Elias & Ryan, 2011; Frankowski & Clark, 2009), and thus the relationship and intimacy needs of sexual and gender minorities remain largely unknown and unacknowledged.

Another complex issue is residents of aged care facilities engaging with sex workers. In places where sex work is legal, residential care facilities of all kinds are faced with the challenge of whether to make sex workers available to their residents. Some facilities make sex workers available – either by transporting residents to commercial premises, or making space available within the facility. Few if any facilities will advertise this fact in their publicity materials (We have croquet! Spa and swimming pool! Sex workers!). Some facilities, of course, would not consider such a possibil-ity, citing moral or practical obligations, and risk. How much of the life of a resident is private, and how much is subject to agency control? What is the right of the resident to experience sexuality and intimacy, and what is the obligation of the facility to facilitate it? What is the actual risk to the organisation? As long as safer sex practices are implemented to avoid sexually transmitted infections (which would apply in any case), there seems to be little actual risk to the resident, and probably some benefit. Person-centred care would suggest that it is the residents, not the staff, who should make these kinds of decisions, yet it is the staff (who may also be responding to family members) who end up making such decisions. These are the challenges facing contemporary residential facilities, and as an Internet-savvy population cohort – one with quite different attitudes towards sexuality and intimacy than their parents – ages into residential care, these complexities will become more acute. These issues, of course, are not limited to aged care facilities, but have implications for residential care of all kinds.

As we saw in the case of Henry and Donna above, sexuality and intimacy in residents with dementia in aged care facilities are a particular challenge because the ethical and legal expectations of consent can be difficult to ascertain (Ehrenfeld et al., 1999; Hajjar & Kamel, 2003). Reports of sexual disinhibition in persons living with dementia circulate among staff, yet as we saw in Chapter 3, these reports vary widely. This wide variation is attributed to the lack of a clear definition around this issue: what is sexual disinhibition? If Mr Smith appears to be masturbating in the day room do I put a blanket over him? Ask him to go to his own room? Or, because I have very conservative values, do I file an incident report to demonstrate how shocked I am? In traditional top-down care facilities, staff have more power than residents. In these kinds of facilities, staff regulate the lives of residents, determine when they eat, when they sleep, how to manage their personal hygiene, and so forth. Care staff may be of social and cultural backgrounds that differ from residents and because education around sexuality varies widely from institution to institution, and jurisdiction to jurisdiction, there is wide room for misunderstanding sexual behaviour. The most intimate parts of the lives of residents are therefore subject to the panopticon, constantly under staff supervision and control. Health providers in general do not understand supporting the sexuality and intimacy of their residents or patients as part of their jobs. In addition, as we saw in the case of Henry, Donna, and her daughter, negotiating the sometimes competing interests of residents, staff, families, and regulatory bodies (as well as assumed public opinion) is not simple. Approved protocols will usually manage risk to the institution by avoiding sexuality in the guise of protecting the resident. Yet we know that residential care is marketed mostly to family members, and it is difficult for many children, even mature adult children, to contemplate their parents having sexual feelings of any kind, let alone acting on those feelings. If a person in a legal marriage enters residential care and because of dementia forgets that they are married, what are staff to do when that person begins a new intimate relationship with someone else? How will they respond to the children of these residents? How are the living spouses or the children meant to respond? These practical questions are not theoretical: they are lived and very real challenges that residential care managers and staff must address daily. Care providers can respond from a top-down risk-management perspective, or a wellness-focussed person-centred perspective, and those responses will look quite different.

Categorical imperative

We think the relationships between resident and caregiver, medical staff and patient, worker and client have been shaped by concepts of vulnerability and marginality that established particular kinds of power relationships that are replicated throughout the human services sectors. We have seen that these categories, and managing people as though these categories are real rather than constructed, have very real, and often painful, human consequences. They have led to an exclusively top-down approach that focuses on risk rather than residents. In the next chapter, we shall consider the possibilities of person-centred care with a focus on wellbeing rather than agency risk management. Person-centred approaches work with the strengths and resilience of an individual, rather than their perceived or constructed vulnerabilities. Such approaches are gaining traction in many parts of the world in different health, mental health, and social services sectors. The goal of such approaches is to increase autonomy and self-determination, and to return to the individual the authorship of their own life. We recognise that this concept will be very challenging to policy-makers and managers who are committed to constructions of vulnerability, marginality, and risk management. We think taking this risk will be worthwhile.

Note

1 We may be grateful that the modern state no longer physically brands able-bodied poor ('sturdy beggars') with a 'V' after two-years' enslavement for their first offense as a 'vagabond', puts them to death after their second, as occurred under Edward VI from 1547–1550, or burns them through the ear from 1572 as in the early days of the reign of Elizabeth I. As we saw in Chapter 2, however, prisons have been stretched beyond capacity in neoliberal regimes, and a prison record or tattoo is as effective as any brand in stigmatising the poor.

Key questions for Chapter 5

This chapter has suggested that economic philosophy and political expediency have replaced human beings at the core of social care and human services. These models have created contemporary notions of vulnerability and marginality that focus on risk management rather than the person. We have proposed that these approaches are neither supported by data nor real-world experiences.

- In your opinion, to what extent are intimacy and sexuality private matters, and to what extent are they public ones?
- How do you understand fairness? How do you understand equity?
- Do you think some people are more worthy of public resources than others?
- How can we make social service agencies accountable to clients and residents, families, funders, and the public?
- How do you manage risk in your personal life? How do you manage risk in your professional life? Are you the person who is responsible for managing risk in your professional life, or is there an authority (a governance body or similar) that through policy directs the way you manage risk?
- To what extent should people living with dementias be allowed to make their own decisions about intimate and sexual relationships?

6   Restoring the human to human services

In previous chapters, we have proposed that risk-management and institution-centred models of care can and often do result in inequitable care for individuals. When individuals are constructed as vulnerable, rules and protocols managing both individual care and institutional behaviour are put in place, and then enforced in order to manage the risk that has been created. But identifying the problems (and the contexts that have created them) is only half the challenge. As health and human services practitioners, we must also develop practical solutions. When faced with an individual with a problem, practitioners are faced with the choice of changing the person, changing the environment, or changing the interactions between the person and their environment. Neoliberal and risk-management solutions have attempted to force the person to change by imposing increasingly restrictive environments, often in the guise of increased accountability. In this chapter, we propose the opposite: changing the paradigm of policies, protocols, and practices from one that creates and manages vulnerability to one that encourages the individual to remain an empowered and resilient partner in their own care. We propose restoring the human to human services. Such paradigms have been widely promoted for at least the last decade as variations of 'person-centred care' (PCC), although there are a variety of constructions of this term, and the term itself has been called 'vague' (Morgan & Yoder, 2012). We will below clarify the history and context of PCC and our understanding of PCC as more a process than an outcome.

Claiming to practice as a person-centred practitioner is seductive: not every practice model that calls itself person-centred is truly person-centred, yet such practice models give practitioners the comfort that they are placing the client's interests at the core of the practice relationship. Person-centred approaches recognise that individuals are the only true experts in their own lives. No one, not even an identical twin, has precisely the same experiences in life that I do, and therefore no one can interpret my experiences the way I do. No one else knows 'just how I feel', and no one has had an experience just like mine. I ascribe (or create) meaning to events in my life that are unique to me. Therefore, it is only through meaningful engagement that the care worker can begin to understand the epistemic framework of their client. Person-centred (or family, group, or community-centred) approaches must also take into account that resources are not unlimited. Health and human services practitioners cannot ensure everything a person wants or needs can be provided, even though they may passionately agree that it is in the client's or community's interest. When several patients presents with acute critical renal failure and in desperate need for a kidney transplant, limited availability of donor organs may raise complex discussions about not only who is the most 'worthy' recipient, but also careful negotiations on how best care can be delivered in the absence of a donor organ. Similarly, a community's need for a child-care centre or dementia day care facility may be widely supported, but the resources may not be prioritised for this need. This may require careful negotiation of how best to address the care need in the absence of adequate resources or until such resources can be acquired.

Realistic person-centred care therefore emerges from 'negotiated relationships' (McCormack, 2003), which are part of a hermeneutic dialogue between persons, their care providers, their social environment, and the resources available to them. Such dialogues refocus attention from managing risk to promoting resilience. Person-centred approaches capitalise on and foster resilience. Such a paradigm shift has implications not only for residential and patient care, but also for policy, funding, research, and ethical decision-making about populations and communities that have been marginalised, and have been labelled 'vulnerable'.

History and context of person-centred practice

In the context of health care, PCC has a lengthy history arguably dating back to Florence Nightingale (Lauver et al., 2002, cited in Morgan & Yoder, 2012), where the patient rather than the disease was the focus of the nurse. This concept was extended by Balint to physicians in 1968, and developed by Mead and Bower in 2000 to include five dimensions: a biopsychosocial perspective, patient as person, shared power and responsibility, the therapeutic alliance, and doctor as person (Morgan & Yoder, 2012).

A 2001 British study found that patients strongly wanted a patient-centred approach, with an emphasis on communication, partnership, and health promotion (Little et al., 2001). Characteristics of a medical model of PCC are that it is holistic, individualised, respectful, and empowering; that it includes the health care environment, and its commitment to patients; and organisational attitudes and behaviours, which also include shared governance with staff. These attributes yielded improved quality of care, increased satisfaction with health care, and improved health outcomes (Morgan & Yoder, 2012). 'Patient-centred practice' in medicine and nursing has become distinct from 'person-centred participation' (Thórarinsdóttir & Kristjánsson, 2012); making choices and shared decision-making are fundamental to person-centredness, but not as attributes of participation (p. 3). Fundamental to person-centred participation are the concepts of human connection, respect, and equality. These attributes are not a goal, but the foundation of a person-centred helping relationship.

Person-centred models have entered the care discourse (e.g., Eden Alternative®, n.d.), although they are quite variously interpreted and applied. Carl Rogers (1961) promoted a client-centred[1] notion of counselling and psychotherapy that was adopted by psychology and related disciplines such as social work, which promoted the belief that the client is the only natural authority on him or herself, and that the work of the clinician could best be accomplished through genuine caring, respect, empathy, authenticity, and unconditional positive regard for the client. These notions were readily adapted by social work as foundational skills that form the basis of many different interventions (Hepworth et al., 2016). Client-centred care is also consistent with the core social work values of self-determination and participation. The Rogerian approach has been critiqued as expensive and time-consuming: personal growth is a luxury in an era of 'solution-focussed' and 'task-centred' models that move clients in and through overcrowded and under-resourced agency practices. Nevertheless, at least conceptually, the Rogerian approach forms a part of the background of most mental health practices even today.

PCC requires health and mental health care professionals to "think beyond concepts of cure based on scientific facts and technical competence, to the adoption of a more holistic approach that incorporates values" (McCormack, 2003, p. 203). This recalls René Dubos' often-cited quotation,

> To heal does not necessarily mean to cure. It can simply mean helping people to achieve a way of life compatible with their aspirations – to

restore their freedom to make choices – even in the presence of continuing disease.

(Dubos, 1978)

Concepts of health and mental health are cultural and contextual: they may be shaped by the presence or absence of symptoms, but they may also be shaped by concepts of what is normal or abnormal in a population, or what is statistically most common, and by how the individual is able to perform their social roles, how they conduct their relationships, or how they maintain balance and harmony within themselves and with other people in their social environment. These concepts may also be individual. To impose a singular Western, positivist, 'scientific' standard of health or mental health on an individual may be to impose a standard that is alien and alienating to the individual. This concept is difficult for many Western-trained health and mental health care practitioners for whom the preservation of life is the compelling value. The preservation of life – sometimes regardless of the quality of that life – as the ultimate value is also shaped by a risk-management perspective: the institution (or state) does not want to be responsible for the risks associated with not doing everything possible to preserve life, or at least to prevent death. Here, of course, we are on the verge of complex ethical (and legal) issues that are beyond the scope of this book and have been well considered by others. But we may say that there are times and places where the values of the individual and the values of the care provider, institution, and even policy environment may be dissonant, and that PCC at a minimum requires respect for the individual's right to determine what health and wholeness is for them.

However, entirely person-centred care is an almost unattainable ideal because, in practice, the person can never really have access to unlimited resources, and their knowledge is inevitably limited. A risk for PCC practitioners is that they may think that they are truly honouring the wishes of the individual by creating and offering choices, but offering a choice between the pasta and the fish for dinner and when to eat it creates only the illusion of person-centredness. If the practitioner creates the choices (and therefore retains power to create and offer choice), then is the care truly person-centred? Providing different options of treatment to an individual with complex health needs assumes that the person is capable of understanding the benefits and challenges of each medical intervention, and has both the capacity to make the best decision – sometimes under pressure – and the resources to support the preferred choice. We propose that what is really needed is negotiation with the recipients of care, which must be based in the reality that there are inevitable limits to any individual's freedom, choices, resources, and knowledge of context.

McCormack (2003) proposes this idea of a 'negotiated relationship', and describes a hermeneutical decision-making model. Hermeneutics, or the science and art of interpretation, is a reflexive way of engaging in conversation with another person. It is iterative – that is, it takes place in steps; it is dialogic – that is, it takes place in open-hearted dialogue, or conversation; and it is reflexive – that is, both (or all) individuals in the conversation are open to being changed by the other. We allow ourselves to be truly empathetic to the other person, to be able not only to see the world as they see it, but to understand the world as they understand it (Henrickson, 2005). We seek not merely to achieve an outcome, but to engage in a process to understand the epistemic framework of the other person. To use Buber's language that we introduced in Chapter 1, it treats the other as a 'Thou' rather than an 'It', and we in turn are treated as Thous, rather than Its. Instead of nurse and patient, we are two persons; rather than social worker and client, we are two humans striving to form an authentic relationship that will achieve outcomes desirable to both of us. To allow ourselves to be transformed by the other is a significant personal risk, of course, because we make ourselves vulnerable; we place ourselves on the margins. Yet by making ourselves vulnerable, we share in the vulnerability of the client or patient, and thereby both reduce their isolation and support them to be less vulnerable. By placing ourselves on the margins, we relocate the margins so that they are less marginal. In order to be a Thou, we must be what the existential philosopher Martin Heidegger called 'authentic' (*eigentlich*). Our authentic selves set aside our professional roles (social worker, physician, nurse), and find a way to be fully human in relationships and in the world. We acknowledge that this intimate kind of relationship with persons in our care is not what is taught in medical or nursing programmes (although we hope it is taught in social work courses), and in high-volume contexts (such as emergency departments) it is not always practical or necessary. But when we are in longer term relationships with persons in care, such as with people living with chronic conditions, ageing persons, or persons with disabilities, we propose that authenticity is what is most respectful and most fully human. Authenticity will naturally lead us to person-centred care.

What this kind of authentic relationship does is encourage and maximise resilience. We introduced this concept in Chapter 2. There is no clear and comprehensive definition of this intangible yet most important quality, although there is a growing literature on resilience (see, for instance,

Cohn et al., 2009; Deveson, 2003; Jeffcott, Ibrahim, & Cameron, 2009; Werner, 2005; Windle, 2011). Resilience is not simply about the ability to 'bounce back' from difficulties. Resilience fosters agency. Agency is the ability to influence one's environment, to act effectively. When we are fully and authentically human, we discover agency in others, and ideally help them discover agency in themselves. Individuals have agency when we value them, and do not remove or suppress their agency through policy, protocols, or practice. Resilience models of care build on individual and community strengths rather than on their labelled problems and 'deficits', their diagnoses or problems. Resilience requires a reconceptualisation of the concept of care delivery, and requires experts not merely to share power (after all, if you have the ability to share power or grant permission, you still control all the power), but to reconstruct their ideas of power and expertise. Resilience requires the relocation of power from so-called experts to individuals, their families, and their communities. Being authentically human, reconceptualising power, and building resilience and agency will require that we re-educate professionals to embrace the lived expertise of recipients of care, and to re-educate clients, patients, residents, and other persons in our care to own their expertise. PCC in practice appears a simple thing, but if we begin with PCC practice and follow its implications, it can be transformational. PCC is, therefore, multi-faceted and comprises individual, community, systems, and policy applications.

Person-centred approaches in practice

In the developed world, at least, using 'expert' models of care and positivist science, we have taught persons in our care to be compliant, to respect the expertise of professionals, to follow orders, and to be passive recipients of care. Patients are labelled compliant or non-compliant, adherent or non-adherent to their therapeutic regimens. Similarly, professionals are taught to be the experts, to give orders, and to provide a particular kind of care. With allopathic medical knowledge often privileged over other forms of knowledge, there is a hierarchy of expertise even in the multidisciplinary team of health professionals (Pollard, Thomas, & Miers, 2010) and the recipient of care may be well down the list of experts to be consulted, even though they are at least nominally the most invested person in their care.

Recipients of care

Theorists have challenged this notion of 'expert' care as located in professionals – most noticeably the Chronic Care Model (CCM) developed in the 1990's by Ed Wagner and colleagues (Wagner et al., 2001) and integrated into policies and guidelines in health contexts internationally. This model is based on the philosophy that care can be delivered more effectively and efficiently if patients with chronic conditions take an active role in their own health and wellness and also suggests that transformations in the relationships among health care systems, communities, and patients are required in order to improve health care for those with chronic conditions. There will be many instances across the world where individuals attempt on a daily basis to engage and negotiate with professionals and systems for their own benefit or that of their loved ones: a cancer survivor advocating for controversial interventions to manage the effects of radiation; a mother keeping a detailed diary of the activities of her terminally ill child so as to inform the meeting with the specialist; or children of a parent living with dementia researching cutting-edge interventions and advising less-informed carers. At times of crisis, when we feel most vulnerable, we must let go of our striving for power; only when we gain a sense of wellness does our sense of capacity to negotiate a relationship improve.

A powerful example of communities taking charge of their own care is during the early days of the HIV epidemic, when experts did not know very much about preventing or treating the disease. Marginalised communities, particularly gay men, had to take charge of caring for themselves, and a new understanding of agency (some time later called 'patient advocacy', although it was much more) emerged. In developed nations, communities of sexual and gender minorities learned quite quickly to take care of themselves and those they cared about. Peer models emerged to educate marginalised (and even criminalised) communities of men who had sex with men, injecting drug users, and cis- and transgender sex workers, and these models became globally respected standards, and inclusion of affected communities became the global standard (Joint United Nations Programme on HIV/Acquired Immune Deficiency Syndrome, 1999). In many cases, these peer and community workers did not have a health care background, but they had their life experiences of oppression and marginalisation, and a passion for their communities, and they rapidly learned and kept abreast of emerging developments. Lives were saved, and health care and health education was transformed around the world forever. These communities unquestionably demonstrated resilience, agency, and humanity in ways that traditional public health, health care, and government and its agencies did not, could not, and could not imagine. Not only do we need to learn from the successful examples of people with lived experience taking charge, but also to embrace the benefits of and possibilities for transformation when professionals are educated to work collaboratively in teams that place the person central to the team's focus.

Care teams

As PCC requires a shift from traditional approaches to care to more involvement by the recipients of care, it necessitates a different way of work for professionals. Success is dependent to some extent on how well professionals in this care model can allow open-hearted conversation across traditional boundaries. The challenge to engage successfully in PCC is compounded where a team of professionals is involved. While there has been much written about the benefits of collaboration with professionals being encouraged to work in an interdisciplinary and inter-agency manner, there is growing recognition that they do not always have the skills and experience to enable this to happen (Soklaridis, Oandasan, & Kimpton, 2007). They may furthermore experience a lack of appreciation for what other disciplines or professions do (Hughes & McCann, 2003) and a lack of time to collaborate (Dey, De Vries, & Bosnic-Anticevich, 2011). We suggest this is further influenced by professionals' perceptions of clients or patients' vulnerability and of risk.

When a young carer of a parent needs access to health services on behalf of the parent, a range of care decisions need to be made. A general practitioner may consider the risk of prescribing medication against the condition experienced by the patient and the risk of allowing the young carer to administer it. A pharmacist may consider the risks of the patient taking the medicine in the right dose and possibly in combination with other medications, and may consider the legal risks of dispensing to the carer. Whether they will communicate about their decisions with each other, the carer, the patient, and potentially other disciplines is unclear and probably hindered by systems and policies, as we will consider in a moment. However, in person-centred approaches, the combined expertise of multiple professionals will be included in decisions alongside the needs and expectations of the patient and carer and patients will be encouraged to share in the control of their care. Decisions may be shaped by cultural and contextual factors and what is considered acceptable in their context. This kind of sharing of power and expertise requires the recipients of care to take responsibility for decision making about their own lives, but also of the professionals to develop collegial relationships across disciplines in accessing information and/or facilitating additional assistance for a patient.

There are many contexts where PCC is negotiated successfully and effectively, but for the most part, this negotiation is dependent on individuals' own practice paradigms and how they respond within the constraints of the systems in which they work. A palliative care team, for instance, can fulfil their roles in a traditional way of work by suggesting best end-of-life care options and offering loss and grief counselling, or they can engage in a negotiated relationship to determine what constitutes a 'good death' within the constraints of resources, systems, and policies. This may well include best end-of-life care and counselling, but may also involve decisions about an alternative place of death or gaining access for a beloved animal companion to a hospital ward. When an attempt at person-centred care is ineffective, the individual may still receive good quality care, but will be disempowered to make decisions about their own care. When care teams effectively negotiate care, the individual remains an empowered and resilient partner in their own care – not only in terms of the best medical outcomes, but also in terms of other factors impacting quality of life for that person.

There is evidence to suggest that there may be differences across disciplines in terms of the perceived value of collaboration with other professionals and with the care recipient (Pollard, Thomas, & Miers, 2010). Hierarchical barriers between different professions have also been widely discussed, with the dominance of general practitioners within health teams raised as an issue across a range of professions (Miers, 2010). Tensions in relationships between professionals and care recipients may also be due to an unclear definition of each other's role and responsibility and a lack of understanding of the boundaries of roles. This places a responsibility on educators of human service professionals and professional bodies who determine professional standards of conduct to ensure professionals are able to implement patient-centred approaches.

Systems of care

It appears that even if practitioners were universally to commit themselves to PCC that is iterative, dialogic, and hermeneutic, the systems of care in which they practice may prevent person-centeredness. Bergeson and Dean (2006) propose four changes to the system of care to better allow practitioners to provide care centred on patients' needs and expectations. They call for a system that allows first for open access to and continuity of care with clinicians, and second for improved opportunities for patients and families to participate in the care process. They acknowledge that it is a substantial challenge for patients to have access to an appointment when they want or need it and with the clinician they choose. However, they emphasise that organisations that have done so have seen substantial improvements in patient satisfaction, better utilization of services, and improved staff and physician satisfaction. This access may be creatively managed within a care team more widely and through different methods of patient contact if the boundaries and responsibilities are clearly defined. Providing active self-management support is a third change required to the system of care. Patients need to develop skills and confidence to increase the possibility of participating in their own care and taking more responsibility for their own lives. Collaborative goal-setting and action planning is not something that is embraced by traditional models of physical care (but seen more in mental health care), but will encourage and maximise resilience and foster agency. Lastly, more efficient and reliable mechanisms for coordinating care between settings need to be established. They warn that poor information flow between care settings is frustrating to patients and clinicians alike and reduces safety margins. Such coordination is increasingly effective for patients living with chronic illness. However, it is less so for patients traditionally regarded as vulnerable or perceived as responsible for their own situation, such as those living with HIV, substance misusers, sex workers, or the homeless.

We saw in a previous chapter how institutional policy and practice about intimacy and sexuality in persons in residential care is a vexed issue, yet one that has a direct impact on residential care: one institution responded with legal action in the case of Henry and Donna, who we read about in the previous chapter. We also saw that the literature suggests that policies, practices, and training for those policies vary by jurisdiction and institution, in many cases leaving it up to staff to respond to resident expressions of sexuality based on their own values. Yet there are places where resident sexuality and sexual behaviours are well supported. The Hebrew Home at Riverdale (New York, USA) has publicly posted their policy on sexual expression by residents, which has existed since 1995, and was most recently revised in 2013 (Dessel & Ramirez, 1995/2013). In this policy, the facility "recognizes and respects the importance of emotional and physical intimacy in the lives of older adults. Such close human interactions are viewed as a normal and natural aspect of life" (p. 1). The policy also notes the importance of consent:

> This policy recognizes and supports the older adult's right to engage in sexual activity, so long as there is consent among those involved.

Consent may be demonstrated by the words and/or affirmative actions of an older adult:

a)   with intact decision-making ability; or
b)   with intact decision-making ability who is non-verbal; or
c)   with Alzheimer's disease or Dementia

The policy sets out that consent is an essential component of sexual expression, and that there are a variety of ways that staff can ensure that consent exists in both cognitively intact and cognitively impaired persons. The policy also sets out the expectations of staff and of the facility to support various kinds of sexual expression by residents. In this way, the facility achieves a balance between individual autonomy and rights and also protections to ensure that autonomy and the capacity to assert those rights exists.

Another example of the implications of a person-centred focus of care in quite a different arena is the way HIV testing is being funded and delivered by international non-governmental organisations. We have long known that testing persons at risk for HIV infection is an effective way not only of identifying persons with the virus and encouraging them into appropriate care, but also educating both infected and uninfected persons about prevention of transmission. As a result of the increasing availability of antiretroviral therapies, the World Health Organisation guidelines have encouraged testing and early treatment of anyone with HIV since 2013, as both a treatment and public health prevention intervention. Many nations and regions have taken their lead from the WHO guidelines.

A tension remains, however, about what the goals of HIV testing are, and the best way to achieve the goals of HIV testing. One approach is to offer HIV testing on a voluntary basis (known as voluntary counselling and testing, VCT, or sometimes voluntary confidential counselling and testing, VCCT). VCT has been available in some form since HIV testing became available in the mid-1980s. The goal of VCT has been to encourage people who believed they were at risk for HIV to seek out an HIV counsellor who would provide education about how the individual can reduce their risk of acquiring HIV through safer sex or drug use practices, and then for the counsellor to offer HIV testing as a part of a risk reduction strategy. The VCT counsellor and client together devise a risk reduction strategy that is tailored to the client's specific needs and risks. Another approach, often called provider initiated testing and counselling (PITC), is to routinise HIV testing for certain classes of persons (e.g., women in antenatal care) in order to screen a wider proportion of the population.

In this model, it is proposed, although patients are nominally offered a choice, testing will be far more common, and more people will be encouraged into appropriate therapies earlier in the course of HIV infection. This is thought to be particularly important to prevent mother to child transmission of HIV *in utero* and during birth. Patients must choose *not* to be tested. In theory, of course, the counselling associated with the testing is provided, but in practice, a comprehensive risk assessment and the range of education and skills may not be offered because the goal of the intervention is the HIV test result. VCT works with individuals to develop risk reduction skills and strategies, while PITC works to encourage people into antiretroviral therapies. Which of these models is more person-centred? Is a person-centred approach the best approach in this instance? We propose, of course, that educating and equipping patients, residents, and clients to make good decisions for themselves in the long term is the best approach, but such a strategy requires adequate resources – funding, staffing, time, and materials – that may not be available in critical areas.

Policy and funding

Person-centred approaches can apply not only to health and mental health care, but also to public policy and funding. Person-centred social welfare policy would not problematise individuals but encourage resilience by building on individual and community strengths. PCC in the public policy arena will require a philosophical and policy shift by neoliberal governments, which, as we have proposed, have capitalised on vulnerability in order to control populations. We saw in the previous chapter that central and state governments around the world have imposed increasing restrictions like drug testing on welfare beneficiaries in order to create the impression that they are doing something proactive about poverty; we also saw that such testing is largely political theatre, and certainly not cost-effective. Nevertheless, the public impression that beneficiaries as a group are misusing their benefits has been created. What would happen if public welfare policy restored the human back into human services, services that would then capitalise on resilience and fostered autonomy, rather than a control and compliance model? What would happen if medical models of care ceded expertise to the person rather than the professional? Such changes would disrupt decades if not centuries of privileging certain professions and skills; it would require moving beyond positivist notions of care.

Such changes would also mean that politicians would need to relinquish control over vulnerable and marginalised persons. These changes would require significant education of the public to learn to take responsibility for decision-making about their own lives. It would likely involve a true paradigm shift that has implications for human services throughout societies. Yet such a shift is possible. Economic and social welfare models such as basic income models, which have been around for 600 years, are being reconsidered (Basic Income Earth Network, n.d.) and global economists are rethinking neoliberal economic policy that conserves vulnerability and contributes to widening income disparity (Ostry, Lougani, & Furceri, 2016). Clearly, changing the paradigm of care from a risk-management to a person-centred (or even negotiated) care model would not be easy, and would require initial expenditures and significant retraining of care staff. Yet the possibilities of individuals participating in their own care and taking more responsibilities for their own lives is entirely consistent with the 'less government more individual responsibility' philosophies of governments that support these policies. Person-centred care has significant implications for research and ethical decision making in research, which will be considered in the following chapters.

Note

1 Person-centred care, patient-centred care, client-centred care, individualised care, resident-centred care, person-directed care, and similar terms such as recovery model, enablements, and co-designed care are all considered to refer to the same basic concept (Morgan & Yoder, 2012), but the taxonomy varies according to disciplines and contexts.

Key questions for Chapter 6

This chapter has proposed that person-centred approaches are an important way to return human beings to the centre of social care and human services. These approaches are strength-based and build on resiliency. Such approaches have implications not only at the individual or micro level, but also at the public policy or macro level. Implementing these approaches would challenge many preconceptions and stereotypes, and also the very ways these services are designed, managed, and delivered.

- To what extent should practitioners, in assisting an individual with a problem, get involved in changing the environment rather than changing the person? What are the challenges and benefits of such a focus?
- How can we best manage the situations where the values of the individual and the values of the care provider, institution, and policy environment may be dissonant?
- If you were making decisions about HIV prevention and care, would you choose to focus on working with an individual to develop an individualised risk prevention strategy? Or would you choose to provide HIV testing with a goal to encouraging persons with HIV to get into treatment as soon as possible? What is the basis and rationale of your decision?
- Do you think professionals should respect an individual's right to determine what health and wholeness is for them? How should professionals respond when an individual chooses a course of care that is very different from the professional's understanding?
- To what extent do you think persons in our care can 'unlearn' to be compliant and respect the expertise of professionals above their own needs and expectations? What is required to facilitate that?

7 Practice research with vulnerable and marginalised communities

It will be clear from the discussion in previous chapters, the words 'vulnerable' and 'at risk' are often used interchangeably, with the implication that vulnerable persons are at risk of something that will negatively impact their physical or emotional wellbeing. These perceptions are reinforced by certain practices and discourses that extend to a research context. Many care professionals are involved in research and consider it their professional and ethical obligation to engage in evidence-informed practice. This may result in some professionals engaging in research as consumers of research, but others may be collaborators in the design or implementation phases, as active practitioner-researchers conducting (relatively) small-scale projects in the workplace or for advanced qualifications, or as contributors to research-related activities. In some instances, professionals may be engaged in research as service users, as will be discussed more below. Either way, even if they are not directly involved in research, every care professional can appreciate the importance of research literacy when accessing scientific and scholarly material in their fields of expertise. As such, we consider this chapter and the next, with a focus on practice research, as core to the practice of care professionals and core in re-conceptualising vulnerability and marginality.

Social research by its nature involves people: researchers and members of research teams, employers, colleagues (fellow researchers or practitioners from various disciplines), funders, policymakers, ethics reviewers, human participants, and the intended beneficiaries of the research. The latter group will (and should) include those people who experience vulnerability and marginality, as the field and subjects of inquiry will often be directed at those who are likely to be affected by its outcomes, and may well be directly involved in its processes. This implies that multiple, inter-related research relationships exist in conducting and advancing social research, but the nature of these relationships are impacted by classifications of people who have traditionally been regarded as vulnerable. This chapter will examine the relationships with individuals and communities regarded as experiencing vulnerability and marginality and consider ways to include and protect their participation in research.

Collaborative approaches

Current approaches in social research encourage research that gets close to practice and is empowering in nature for those affected by the findings. The relationship between researchers and participants traditionally involves 'experts' posing questions they formulated for or about individuals and communities, and eventual dissemination of the knowledge they created to users – with an expectation that it will be embraced and adopted. Most recently, the practice-research paradigms have included evidence-based practice (EBP), evidence-informed or evidence-influenced practice, and its many critiques – some of which have had a real impact on the notion of collaboration.

The main tenets of the evidence-based movement are that professional interventions should be based on research findings about 'what worked' and that research should reflect these concerns and form the basis of professional training and practice (Corby, 2006). This was initially widely embraced. However, in the US in particular, the focus on evidence-based practice became highly quantitative and science-based, in that randomised controlled trials were positioned as the gold standard of evidence-based practice, and any other attempts at evidence were seen as of lesser value. This by default resulted in a weakening of evidence obtained in a qualitative paradigm and limited collaboration with stakeholders – as will be discussed more below. Some authors became highly critical of this evidence-based movement, emphasising its methodological weaknesses for practice and poor fit with the complexities inherent in practice (Hammersley, 2005; Webb, 2001). Alternatives such as evidence-informed or evidence-influenced practice that allow for notions of practice wisdom were proposed (Gilgun, 2005), but proponents of evidence-based practice continued to advocate for randomised controlled trials and experimental designs, claiming it as the only rational, science-based activity and a moral obligation (Gambrill, 2003; Thyer, 2004). Gray, Plath, and Webb (2009) provide a comprehensive and analytical discussion of the nature of evidence-based practice and its many debates and interpretations, concluding that it is a subject fraught with controversy. Not surprisingly, then, there has been a good deal of spirited debate both for and against evidence-based practice. This debate is not the focus of this discussion. What is important for us is how researchers and practitioners position themselves in these debates, what they agree is evidence-based practice, and their commitment to collaborative research approaches.

The contemporary view about collaborative and strength-based approaches to research encourages interconnectedness, a shared responsibility for appraising existing knowledge, and creating, validating, disseminating, and adopting knowledge. Practitioner research is regarded as a collaborative effort by a range of stakeholders to advance understanding of practice issues and to make a difference to practice (Fouché, 2015). It is driven by a focus on accountability to service users; emphasises partnerships between practitioners and researchers; supports easier access to data; promotes the dissemination of research findings in easy-to-understand formats; and focuses on outcome issues in practice (Epstein, 2001; Shaw, 2005). Increasingly, funders around the world expect more active user participation in research. The involvement of participants and intended beneficiaries of the research in shaping its focus has become a key principle of 'research that creates change' (Munford & Sanders, 2003). This was partly driven by the 'Nothing about us without us!' campaigns that averred that no policy should be decided without the participation of members of the groups affected by that policy. The term came into use in disability activism during the 1990s, but has since moved from the disability rights movement to other interest groups, including the mental health sector.

Various research methodologies have developed over the years to ensure a scientific and robust process for such collaborative efforts. Collaborative research manifests itself in different participatory research strategies with each type driven by specific characteristics related to the real or perceived nature of participation. These include

- action research (AR);
- participatory learning and action (PLA) or participatory action research (PAR), where the activity is positioned as simultaneously a form of inquiry and a form of practical action (Stringer, 2014);
- community-based participatory action research (CBPR) or asset-based community development (ABCD), where it is posed that the community (however that is defined) participates fully in all aspects of the research process beyond dissemination to application (Mayan & Daum, 2015);

- appreciative inquiry (AI), where the impetus is on the cooperative search for the best in people, their organizations, and the world around them in the implementation of a participatory design (Reed, 2007); and
- participatory rural appraisal (PRA), where the knowledge and opinions of rural people are deliberately incorporated in the planning and management of projects (Kemmis & McTaggart, 2005; Reason & Bradbury, 2008).

Practices that are collaborative and empowering in nature have also been introduced in traditional methodologies such as evaluation research through developmental or empowerment evaluation, which is aimed at helping communities monitor and evaluate their own performance (Fetterman, Kaftarian, & Wandersman, 2014; Patton, 2011).

Levels of engagement

If collaborative efforts seem to be increasingly valued by service users, policy-makers, funders, and at least some researchers, they raise the question of how best to ensure authentic collaboration. Collaboration and engagement are complex constructs that have generated a proliferation of material in recent popular and academic literature. The discussions reflect different contexts such as organisational engagement, community engagement, or social media engagement and a focus on different populations, such as employees, students, and patients. Irrespective of these differences, many authors present engagement as a continuum or a process that develops incrementally across different levels. Distinctions are drawn between informing, consulting, involving, collaborating, and co-leading or empowering.[1] This framing of engagement can usefully be applied to research where contemporary and post-modernist approaches increasingly embrace and even encourage the role of the researcher in fieldwork. However, as long ago as the early 1990s, it was noted that even in collaborative efforts, researchers fail to view practitioners as full partners in research (Galinsky et al., 1993). That remains true today.

In traditional positivist research paradigms, there are clear boundaries in terms of researchers' level of engagement in the field. Positivist paradigms set out the expectation of objectivity, that is, for the researcher to distance themselves from the data and any contamination of the findings. This often results in engagement that is limited to informing or consulting various stakeholders, and may involve a level of collaboration that is limited to including stakeholders as a reference group or as participants in the research. Researchers select topics and designs that are of interest to them – sometimes driven by funding priorities determined by those in power – and implement those with the support of a practice community under the banner of collaborative research. However, where the research question is set by the researcher (or funder), collaboration is 'contaminated' from the outset, irrespective of the level of engagement that follows, as only data relevant to the researcher's question is canvassed and analysed. Furthermore, in many settings, practitioners become collaborators in research by merely being data collectors, or providing access to participants. Collaborative research that reaches the level of co-leading or empowerment is limited, but there are excellent examples of various stakeholders working together in shaping topics and designs, jointly implementing these and interpreting and disseminating findings in ways that value multiple expertises.[2] The relationship between the researcher or research team and those who are 'researched' is fundamental; the more collaborative the research, the more fundamental the relationships. These forms of advanced engagement are not without its challenges though.

Research relationships are impacted by our perceptions and notions of vulnerability. Once we define individuals or communities as vulnerable, the approach, engagement, and relationship is shaped by these definitions. In the process, so-called vulnerable and marginalised people can be excluded from research in order to 'protect' them, thereby potentially creating more risk than their careful inclusion in research. A project on guidelines for caregivers in dealing with intimacy and sexuality in people living with dementia, utilising collaborative approaches, will be very different if we consider this population as vulnerable participants in research, or as a risky topic for research, as opposed to partners in an inquiry leading to practical action (action research) or collaborators in a cooperative search for the best in people, their organizations, and the world around them (appreciative inquiry). In overmanaging the safety of participants, we potentially exclude them from participation in well-meaning attempts to protect them. We also then exclude their voices from findings that inform policies and practices – often about them, or at the very least impacting them.

Not only is access to populations impacted by definitions and conceptualisations of vulnerability, but the very topics investigated are shaped by these perceptions. If some of the partners in the collaborative research endeavour are regarded as vulnerable or potentially harmed by research activities, it changes both the questions researchers would ask and the answers they will solicit. For instance, in some contexts, it will be impossible to conduct research on sexual and gender matters with young people, not because we consider the potential participants as vulnerable, but because decision-makers may find such projects 'risky' for managerial, political, or ethical reasons (the latter to be considered in more detail in the next chapter). Risk-aversion – or aversion to perceived risk, whether or not it is actual risk – is setting agendas in its own way. By prioritising the focus on and management of risk, the implication is that the information we can obtain (or could have obtained if we were not avoiding risk) is regarded as of lesser importance. One universal example is the avoidance of a focus on the sexual activity of 12-year olds. Restrictions around doing research on this important topic is padded in the risk-averse dialogue that any conversations of such a sexual nature with young people may 'put ideas in their heads'. However, the statistics related to sexually transmitted diseases, abortions, and teenage pregnancies make it glaringly obvious that teenagers do not need researchers to put any ideas about sexual activity in their heads, but rather that the young people may have some powerful stories and experiences to share. This risk-averse approach fails to recognise that most individuals are resilient, capable of engaging in hard conversations that affect their daily lives and in managing the nature of those conversations. In another example of how politics shape research, in 1996, the US Congress, pressured by the National Rifle Association, stripped funding for research on gun violence by the Centers for Disease Control (Hiltzik, 2014; Lowes, 2014), and enacted the so-called 'Dickey Amendment', which forbade the CDC to spend federal funds "to advocate or promote gun control". Since that time, the CDC has taken the politically expedient course of not carrying out any research on gun violence in the US, despite very public attention to the issue in the media. This is a clear and compelling example of how political agendas directly affect research, and thus the lives and deaths of people.

Research on or with 'vulnerable' and 'marginal' populations

There are different ways and levels of including the voice of communities, service users, and particularly groups traditionally perceived as vulnerable and marginalised in research: some relate to openness about and permission to engage in previously unexplored topics or topics with a different focus, some about the inclusion of service users in research, and others about encouraging service users as researchers or researchers to document experiences as service users.

Unexplored topics

It is people in power (including researchers and academics) who decide what and who should be researched. Funding agencies and organisations determine research priorities and influence research agendas and directions. In fact, most academic research priorities are set directly or indirectly by governments. Yet, research findings are rarely used to hold people in power accountable, as officials are not required to take research findings into account when making policy or resourcing decisions. In some contexts, the very opposite may be true, in that researchers may need to obtain permission from funders or commissioners of research to publish their work. An extreme example of this is unfolding in England within the wide-ranging Export Control Bill (Department for Business Innovation & Skills and Export Control Organisation, 2012). As drafted, the bill demands that scientists in a wide range of fields must have their research findings approved by officials before they publish them in scientific journals. The British government is also seeking to keep a list of sensitive subjects under continuous review, and to add technologies or subjects as it sees fit. This will no doubt have a huge impact on the availability of reliable evidence about certain populations and topics. We can only hope that sanity will prevail, as similar restrictive regimes have been dropped in countries such as the US, after they proved to be unworkable. Rossi, Lipsey, and Freeman (2004) use a courtroom analogy to explain that the use of research findings in practice is akin to calling a witness for testimony; lawyers will never call expert witnesses whose testimony might damage their case. Similarly, governments, agencies, managers, and frontline professionals are unlikely to consider research evidence in decision-making if that evidence contradicts their view of the world or disrupts a comfort zone or a business model that is well resourced.

Various contextual factors, including a rise in marginalised persons themselves becoming researchers and decision-makers, or becoming more vocal on matters affecting themselves and their immediate circle of influence, have seen a distinct change in the type of topics being investigated. These changes are as wide-ranging as the fields of inquiry, but some shifts are more obvious. Women's issues were not worthy of exploration in the 1970s and 1980s, but subsequently developed as an entire field of study (Berkin, Pinch, & Appel, 2005). In the years after the initial devastation of HIV/AIDS highlighted the 'vulnerability' of sexual and gender minority communities, queer studies emerged to balance that perceived vulnerability and to highlight the strengths and resiliency of those communities

(Beemyn & Eliason, 1996; Sedgwick, 1990). Historically, the period between childhood and adulthood has been considered a problematic period of developmental disturbance. However, during the late 1990s and early 2000s, a new strength-based approach was introduced aimed at redefining adolescents as "resources to be developed rather than as problems to be managed" (Lerner, Jacobs, & Wertlieb, 2005, p. 3). Research on older people followed similar trends. Focussed mostly on loneliness, isolation, and elder abuse, research on ageing shifted from deficit to strength models with the recent focus on positive ageing, including re-ablement and restorative services and experiences for older people (Jeste & Palmer, 2013). There is also a distinct shift to research on more sensitive topics, including those related to sexuality, intimacy, abortion, euthanasia, religion, and racism. Researchers are encouraged to critically reflect on the factors impacting their decision of research topics and those important social issues that remain unexplored for reasons of risk, power, and privilege.

The inclusion of service users in research

Gaining access to service users for research purposes – both as participants and as members of reference groups, has traditionally been difficult. However, in recent times, these populations are demanding to be heard and included in research; much of this pressure is coming from communities that have been active advocates for this change over many decades, such as consumers of mental health services and indigenous populations. A significant pool of literature has developed around evidence of the inclusion of service users or reference groups in research, the challenges with such research, and of other successful models. The debate surrounding service user involvement seems to have moved beyond arguments about whether service users have a right to be involved or have anything at all useful to contribute to issues about the how, when, and where of involvement. As Beresford and Carr state, "User involvement has had an impact on research as well as becoming a subject of study" (2012, p. 12). In this context, motivations, expectations, roles, and responsibilities of reference groups or service users in a research project should be clearly determined at the outset.

Where service users have usually been passive recipients of care and treatment, a much wider and coherent range of voices are speaking out and are being heard – both individually and collectively. One of the motivations for service users to be involved in research is a desire for an anticipated valid contribution as a result of experiential knowledge

(Jordan et al., 2015). It is accepted that people want to get involved in research to enable change for themselves or for others like them and that practice and policy can benefit from those insider experiences. Researchers do indeed include service user groups and reference groups with the aim to help them consider their assumptions and contextualise the knowledge created from the data (Moore, Noble-Carr, & McArthur, 2016). However, the definition of service users for purposes of research poses a significant challenge, and impacts the type and level of participation in which they are invited to engage.

Health research (and particularly mental health research) most commonly includes service users. Even though contentious at times, research with health and mental health populations is more advanced in this regard than research with populations such as ethnic minorities, prisoners, the poor, and the homeless, where there is silence on the inclusion of service users in research (other than as participants). In writing about the role of users of psychiatric services in service development, Campbell (2001) points out that the service user of today is in a very different position to the mental health patient of the 1960s and 1970s, but comments that the changes of the past 15 years have been in influence rather than control. He notes that "Working together, common concerns and partnership have been important words and phrases that have animated projects but helped conceal some of the realities – the different agendas and the imbalances in power" (2001, p. 88). The question that should be asked is: to what end do we include service users or reference groups in research?

Service users are asked to share views and experiences of a particular design/intervention/topic, but are rarely consulted on preferences and priorities. They may more readily be involved in data collection, but less so in data analysis. There are good reasons for that. On the one hand, universities, research institutions, funders, and governments encourage the greater involvement of service users in research, but on the other hand, prioritise 'expert' views, defined as those with scientific or academic standing. They embrace collaborative approaches, but do not allow adequate time for relationship building. Funders rarely allocate money to engage with service users, but would expect consultation with service users or reference groups on funded projects. They expect proposals and designs that eliminate the element of unknown and in the process, inhibit a real contribution by service users to shape the direction of the research. This again points to the role of those in power shaping the direction, impact, and input of service users in research. Although collaboration is a notion that is widely embraced, there are clear differences in the agenda, objectives, and power of researchers and service users in enacting different models of research. Both researchers and service user participants are trapped in traditional research paradigms and expectations, to the disadvantage of both.

Service users as researchers

Some individuals from populations regarded as vulnerable and marginalised are becoming researchers themselves and starting to produce meaningful data from their lived experiences or perspectives as a service user. There are many practice examples of survivors of suicide, rape victims, paedophiles, ex-gang members, prisoners, parents under investigation for child abuse, and people living with terminal illness, eating disorders, or depression demanding to be heard or researching their own communities. But the scientific literature about this is scarce. Increasingly, we are also experiencing these so-called vulnerable populations in dual roles, as service users and professionals: health professionals, social workers, or counsellors as victims of rape, living with eating disorders, chronic or life-threatening diseases, with complicated grief, in situations of domestic violence, or as caregivers for older adults or disabled youth, as migrants or refugees. These individuals are all able to provide research data from a unique perspective. Often these experiences are shared anecdotally, in social media, or in support groups. But increasingly, these experiences are also being shared in more academic ways (see Bray & McLean, 2015). This may well impact service delivery. There is nothing like a health practitioner being admitted to the hospital or having to support a family member through a public health admission to raise awareness of challenges in the system. However, the range of experiences that fall within acceptable boundaries of disclosure or as research topics are limited and determined by perceptions of vulnerability. A professional can be seen to be enriched by experiences of loss and grief, illness or immigration, but the risk to patients or clients are questioned when these experiences include mental illness, addiction, imprisonment, or abuse, suggesting that some types of vulnerability, marginality, or risk are more acceptable than others as a credible voice in research.

In this chapter, we have proposed that the power relationships that develop from definitions of vulnerability and marginality impact the nature of social research. This influence includes not only the topics researched, but also the research relationships we develop, and are allowed to develop.

Collective approaches to research and increased levels of engagement with various groups of people are encouraged. We argue that inclusion and protection of various individuals' and communities' participation in research are dependent on the re-conceptualisation of categories of vulnerability. In the next chapter, we shall consider how the conceptualisation of vulnerability shapes the relationship with committees responsible for ethical approval of research projects and how the competence, values, resourcing, and culturally informed impressions of the review committee members impact the application of risk and vulnerability guidelines. It is essential that new strategies to ensure ethical conduct in practice that allow for a different awareness and representation of vulnerability and risk are developed and implemented.

Notes

1 These distinctions are often based on models developed by the well-known Tamarack Institute (http://tamarackcci.ca/) or by the International Association for Public Participation (www.iap2.org/).
2 See examples from the Social Care Workforce Research unit: www.kcl.ac.uk/sspp/policy-institute/scwru/index.aspx

Key questions for Chapter 7

Research is important because it shapes the ways communities of people are understood, and it helps funders as they set research priorities. This chapter has begun to consider the implications of current notions of vulnerability and marginality to research, including the ways research is funded, conceptualised, and carried out by researchers. It has also suggested greater engagement with so-called vulnerable and marginalised communities in research.

• Do you think collaborative approaches to research can be embraced with all communities or are there some populations you would exclude from such approaches? Why?
• What are the factors impacting your decision of research topics? Are there any important social issues in your view that remain unexplored for reasons of risk, power, and privilege?
• Do you think some populations more than others can be included as a reference group in research? Why?
• Do you have a dual role as professional and service user? Are you prepared to speak publicly about this dual role? What would you like your listeners to know?
• To what extent should service users be allowed to shape research agendas and findings?

8   Research ethics

Perceptions about the relationship between the researcher and the researched outlined in the previous chapter are extended in this chapter to include a focus on the relationship with committees responsible for ethical approval of research projects. For some care professionals, contact with research ethics committees may seem to be restricted to projects undertaken under the auspices of universities for advanced qualifications. The relationship with these committees is indeed a crucial part of university researchers' and postgraduate students' research journeys. However, it is foolish to think that practitioners and service users are not affected by this relationship. As will become clear in this chapter, the boundaries of ethical conduct shape the way projects are conceptualised, designed, implemented, and disseminated. This ethical conduct in turn determines not only the type and reliability of evidence, but significantly impacts both professionals and service users as participants in and consumers of research. The impact becomes particularly pronounced when we consider how notions of vulnerability and marginality impact ethical conduct. As such, consideration of research ethics is not the exclusive domain of university researchers, but core to the person-centred practice of care professionals and the experiences of service users.

Human research ethics committees (HRECs), institutional review boards (IRBs), research ethics boards (REBs), research review committees (RRCs), and ethical review boards (ERBs) (all referred to as ethical review committees [ERCs] for the purpose of this discussion) are appointed to approve and apply the ethical guidelines through which research is implemented. ERCs are charged with the responsibility for ensuring that research conducted under the auspices of their institutions is carried out ethically. There is no doubt that ethical review is necessary to safeguard participants, and particularly the absolutely vulnerable, regarded as those participants who are especially disempowered, helpless, or at risk of harm or exploitation. But there is some tension in terms of how members of ERCs fulfil their roles and especially how they perceive and apply risk and vulnerability guidelines. Researchers often find it difficult to design research with populations defined as vulnerable and marginalised that will satisfy and get approval from ERCs. Furthermore, using collaborative research designs with such communities will not only make it difficult to meet the expectations of ERCs, but an unanticipated set of ethical issues may emerge that need different consideration. So it is important to consider how research ethics and the relationship between researchers, research participants, and ERCs are managed in terms of the potential impact on communities defined as vulnerable and marginalised.

The role of ethics committees

Ethical review is widely acknowledged as an important and necessary process. Regardless of discipline or research philosophy, researchers based at universities, health care settings, or government-funded agencies are required to obtain ethical approval from ethical review committees for projects with human participants. There can be absolutely no doubt that these standards are needed to allow due consideration of the effects of research on participants and participant communities. The complex challenge of negotiating ethical practices is central to any research inquiry. For the most part, decisions about ethical conduct relates to competence. If every researcher were trustworthy, there would be no need for ERCs. But too often, researchers are blinded by their own agendas or are not competent to conduct complex research. ERCs have the responsibility to prevent bad research conducted by incompetent researchers. ERCs have a responsibility not only to safeguard so-called vulnerable participants, but also to ensure researcher competence. The problem comes when ERCs overstep that balance. It is not *that* ERCs need to consider the notions that are critiqued in this chapter, but *how they conceptualise* vulnerability in considering participant recruitment, participation, and consent.

Historic practices

The need for protections of human participants in research emerged as a result of historical abuses perpetrated against human subjects in the name of scientific advancement (Becker, 2005; Guta, Nixon, & Wilson, 2013). As mentioned in an earlier chapter, one of the most prominent documents that influenced ethical review practices is the *Nuremberg Code* (Nuremburg Code, 1949). Realising that there was no international law differentiating between legal and illegal human experimentation, physicians who had worked with the prosecution during the Nuremberg trial outlined six points to the United States Counsel for War Crimes in an attempt to define legitimate research. These were later revised to ten and became known as the *Nuremberg Code* – a set of research ethics principles that continue to serve as a cornerstone for modern regulations regarding the use of human participants in experimentation. Other core codes and guidelines include the Declaration of Helsinki 1964–2000 (World Medical Association, 1964/2013), the Belmont Report 1979 (National Commission for the Protection of Human Subjects of Biomedical and Behavioral Research, 1979), and the Council for International Organizations of Medical Sciences (CIOMS) and World Health Organization (WHO) International Guidelines (Council for International Organizations of Medical Sciences, 1982, 1993, 2002). This last, while retaining the spirit of the *Nuremburg Code*, condensed the ten ethics principles to three: beneficence, justice, and respect for persons (Cuigini, 2015), and these are increasingly used in ethical guidelines internationally. Beneficence refers to the obligation to maximize benefits and minimize harm. It implies a consideration of the probability that certain harm will occur to subjects from participation in research. Justice aims to protect populations from exploitation and suggests an obligation to treat each person equitably and equally and avoid conflicts of interest. Respect for persons implies respect for a person's ability to make sound decisions and to enable them to analyse the risks associated with proposed participation, which denotes respect for participants' privacy and allow them informed and voluntary consent.

Ethical guidelines arising from these principles are developed by high level committees and for the most part firmly guided by a biomedical framework. This is not surprising given that the worst treatment of research participants has historically occurred in the context of biomedical research, such as came to light during the Nuremberg trials. If we base our decisions about current research ethics on the fear that the most atrocious practices in memory might be repeated, it may cause an overreaction to the point that self-determination is not an option. These guidelines are particularly befitting to projects that are characteristically individualistic, agenda-driven, and outcome-guided. However, decisions about ethical conduct are to a large extent interpreted contextually. Decisions are influenced by ERC members' own values and their culturally informed impressions of what defines beneficence, justice, and respect for persons, and by implication, notions of vulnerability and marginality. Guidelines are furthermore developed on a historically shared understanding of a certain group of people's values and what they think should be done (or not) to certain categories of people. For the most part, these individuals, groups, or committees would have comprised White/European cisgendered heterosexual Western male researchers. This inherent bias has left out a number of worldviews on regulations regarding the use of human participants in experimentation.

Projects underpinned by values of flexibility and adaptability, which underscore collaborative approaches, create a tension with these ethical guidelines and for ERCs. This is particularly pertinent when stakeholders' contributions in collaborative research projects are assessed based on these notions of vulnerability and marginality. Bradley articulates this very powerfully by stating that ERCs "can, and often do, silence the voices of the marginalized and perpetuate an academic political economy and a traditional top-down research and professional model that quantify and objectify human lives by keeping them nameless, faceless, and voiceless" (2007, p. 341). There is an irony in this practice, though, in that practitioners conducting research in their own agencies (that are separate from university, health, or government-funded agencies) are largely unable to access ethical review processes. They may by default have access to management entities or boards of governance that will fulfil the task of ethics review – mostly without any experience or knowledge about what they are reviewing. These research practices have escaped the non-negotiable place of ERCs in the protection of human participants in scientific experimentation for decades without any known dire consequences. Innovative responses, such as the New Zealand Ethics Committee (n.d.), to cite a country-specific example, are developing to support the many research projects from professional and community researchers that fall outside the realm of standing ERCs. These grassroots review initiatives may well inform a model for ethical review that embrace collaborative and practice-based research practices.

Risk of harm

As far as risk of harm is concerned, ERCs may be overcautious in attempting to protect vulnerable populations, and effectively discourage researchers from conducting valuable research projects. Researching children is the most common point in case. There are many measures in place to protect vulnerable children from harm through participation in research, including requiring consent from parents or caregivers and putting limitations on activities or topics of discussion. As such, researchers tend to include only participants in certain age groups (i.e., the age set by ERCs as a more acceptable level of vulnerability – usually around 14 or 16 years) and to limit the topics they explore with this vulnerable population. This may partly be the reason for the invisibility of young people's views on topics such as disasters, abuse, transgendered identity, under-aged sexual activity, or living with siblings or parents experiencing live-threatening illness, disability, addiction, or mental illness.

Consequently, there are significant lacunae in knowledge about these important topics for populations of young people. It seems logical that a young person may embrace the opportunity to have a dedicated anonymous discussion about their experiences with an attentive adult or researcher. Certainly, they could be offered the opportunity. The involvement of young participants in research will be aimed at generating desperately needed end-user-generated evidence to inform policies and practices and help increase understanding of issues pertinent to this group of people, including sexuality diversity, teenage pregnancy, or lived experiences of grief and loss, to name but a few. But it may take a fair bit of convincing of an ERC that such research can be carried out respectfully and without causing harm to the young person – especially if we consider the absence of parental consent as highlighted below. Similarly, decisions about the vulnerability of people living with dementia or those with intellectual disabilities have become progressively conventional, discounting individuals who would not only *not* suffer harm, but could possibly benefit from participation in research. Lange, Rogers, and Dodds (2013) suggest that this approach to vulnerability both allows and forces us to look beyond the often procedural issues of harm to individuals to broader issues, including the structure of the research enterprise, or the shape and direction of the research agenda itself.

Most concerning in this deficit and risk-focussed paradigm is the assumption that participants do not have the freedom to refuse participation – which in itself introduces a power imbalance. This paradigm fails to conceptualize the potential participants of research as individuals with understandings, agencies, and competencies in their own lives, and who can, therefore, identify potential risks of research to themselves at least as well if not better than any ERC (Martin, 2007). Members of ERCs therefore become gatekeepers of contextually interpreted ethical guidelines, rather than expert advisors facilitating good, ethical research.

In considering ethical dilemmas in conducting research, researchers may construct an illusion of protection of communities who should be researched by effectively excluding them from real participation. To avoid clashes with ERCs, researchers may deliberately omit certain populations as potential participants, or avoid altogether sensitive topics that anticipate challenging ethics approval processes. Rather than having some kind of meaningful engagement about the ethical challenges, it becomes all too difficult to put safeguards in place that will satisfy people in power. Researchers turn the other way and examine less vulnerable and more accessible communities, or in extreme cases, engage in unethical conduct in practice. In some respects, this tension around research ethics may put research participants and the communities they belong to more at risk than they potentially are. A project where we solicited experiences of people living with HIV highlighted such risks. Some of these participants lived with a real fear of the life-changing implications to themselves and their children if their HIV status were exposed. Many of them refused to put their names on a consent form, and some refused audio-recordings. This was a real ethical dilemma to be managed. They could either be excluded from participation in the study – in which instance their rich experiences were missed (but at least their 'protection' was ensured) – or they may have consented and the well-meaning attempts at managing risk of harm would have exposed them to risk in other places in their lives.

Voluntary and informed consent

Where informed consent is concerned, the challenges for satisfying the expectations of ERCs continue. Research should ordinarily require consent of those involved in a project. It is debatable, though, when and how this consent is obtained, what counts as consent, who benefits from the consent, and at times, whether consent is required at all. When the spontaneous behaviour of children on a public playground or beach is the focus of the investigation, does the researcher require consent? If so, who would provide it and how and when will it be obtained? In an era of easy access to cameras and the sharing of photos, experiences, and information on social media, the nature of data for analysis has changed. Various research projects have a focus on such information that may not necessarily be publicly available, but allow open access to these images to thousands of people. This too raises questions about consent.

In collaborative approaches to research, negotiations for collaboration precede research ethics – sometimes by several months or years. Collaboration may often involve a project of which research is only a small part and in many respects, the researcher may be the one consenting to access participants, data, and premises. Yet, in an institutional ethics review process, informed consent requires the existence of an information sheet and a traditional view of 'subjects' or 'respondents' to consent to the research. A consent form can be seen as representing a legal contract and reaffirms power differentials. It may well jeopardize months of dedication by practitioner researchers to develop a balance in power when community members are required to sign a legalistic document, consenting to a process that they may have perceived as a partnership; this is particularly important where participants come from oral traditions where written documents signal mistrust. For the most part, these community partners comply, based on the trust relationship with the research partners. Voluntary and informed consent then becomes a compliance step, rather than an engagement in ethical conduct.

Increasingly, this requirement to obtain consent from others to reach participants perceived as vulnerable is extended to organisations. Many ERCs require consent forms to be completed by managers or CEOs when members of staff are approached as research participants. One can to some extent understand the rationale if this were to impact on the core business of the organisation, involve staff time or organisational resources, or if staff participation in the project carries reputational risk for the organisation. But not when it is about professional views. A power differential is enforced when teachers, health professionals, and social workers are asked to share their professional views on a topic as research participants, but are unable to do so unless their manager (who may have both limited understanding of the project and their potential participation) consents. Moreover, these processes increasingly expect managers or CEOs to consent that participants will not be disadvantaged for participation or non-participation in the research. Other than the fact that no ERC (or researcher for that matter) will know whether this condition is upheld or not, the procedures for obtaining this consent can also impose unintentional harm, as lack of response from a very busy CEO on matters of relative unimportance may prevent data being collected from key stakeholders. A project was conducted on the views of health professionals about theories and skills required to be effective in a particular context. This topic may be of low importance to a CEO, but may have a crucial impact on the education of the future health care workforce. Excluding certain views, professions, services, or managers due to lack of consent from someone in the hierarchy may cause more harm than the harm we are trying to avoid by introducing this process in the first instance.

Sometimes informed consent from a guardian or caregiver is merely not possible or unrealistic. One would hardly want to ask anyone from an invisible or so-called vulnerable population to obtain informed consent for participation from others who may not be aware of or interested in their status. Minors involved in substance misuse, or an individual who is living with HIV are unlikely to want to get a caregiver to sign a form that they may share their experiences with a researcher. Research with child-headed households for instance involve children at a very young age having to make decisions and take responsibility for much more than whether it is safe to participate in research. Such young people should be allowed to give informed and voluntary consent themselves if the principles of good, ethical conduct are implemented. It seems similarly unrealistic and even unethical to expect a young carer of a disabled or mentally unwell adult to obtain permission from them, or another adult, to participate in research about their experiences, when they independently make life and death decisions about that adult's care on a daily basis. Obtaining consent in writing is potentially problematic for various groups. People living with HIV, mental illness, refugees, sex workers, or women in refuges may not want to put their names on paper in fear of being identified as meeting the criteria for inclusion in research on that particular topic; as noted above, in some cultures, such a process signifies mistrust or a violation of an established trust.

Conflicts of interest

In considering conflicts of interest, one has again to consider the question of 'interests of whom?' In many instances, conflicts of interest involve protection of the perceived vulnerable from people such as researchers and others in a power relationship with the potential participant. This is based on the assumption (and historic evidence) that any population without capacity to arrive at informed decisions on their own accord, such as severely intellectually disabled or mentally unwell or unstable individuals, can potentially be exploited by researchers. Careful consideration of the impact of dual roles and conflicts is therefore crucial. However, this should not be managed as the norm in that any person in a dual role will by default encounter challenges in managing ethical conduct. Collaborative research by its very nature implies the involvement of an insider to the context under study. There are limited options to gain access to some populations' experiences if we are unable to use existing trusting insider relationships to enable this access. The experiences of families in end-of-life conversations with medical staff, of parents of babies born prematurely, or of members of communities involved in illegal activities can very often not be researched by an outsider to that group without significant investment of time and money. No outsider will have the trust and confidence that has been established over a long period of time by hospital staff or practitioners 'on the ground' and in the context. This is also true for teachers wanting to research their own classroom practices or social workers curious about interventions with their own clients, client groups, or communities. Yet these staff may be perceived as having power over these potential participants (raising the possibility of coercion to participate), and therefore potentially conflicting interests. Rather than helping such staff negotiate their roles and interests carefully and compassionately, ethics committees are more likely to impose requirements that exclude these staff from any research role in this context. In fact, it is common practice for ERCs to expect teachers as researchers to replicate any interventions for research purposes with a group outside of their own classroom so as to manage conflicts of interest. The protection of one's 'own' clients to harmful conduct by such a role conflict seems to trump 'good ethical research'.

Ethical conduct in practice

The ethical review process clearly raises questions about partnerships between communities, researchers and ERCs and the unintentional harm that may occur in the process. Debates within the literature question whether the Belmont Report principles (lack of capacity to consent to research; increased susceptibility to coercion or exploitation; and increased risk of harm), as applied by an ERC, are culturally bound and adequate in scope (Shore, 2007). Do we reconsider harm, consent, and conflicts of interest as a contextual issue for some types of projects, or avoid studying certain communities and topics where these issues seem just too difficult to manage? It is important to consider how we define and who defines vulnerability in terms of ethical guidelines and how we balance benefits for participants with 'potential harm' as constructed by ethical review processes. Not all vulnerabilities, of course, are constructed. Some are real, as we have noted in previous chapters, but it is unclear who decides that and on what grounds, for the purposes of research.

Assume a social work practitioner in a hospital setting wants to examine how older people experience the move from living at home, through a hospital admission, to living in residential care. Health professionals work with such individuals every day and will give consideration to elements of beneficence, justice, and respect for the person under their code of professional ethics. However, in a role as researcher, additional consideration is required, including risk of harm, informed and voluntary consent to the research (different from standard practice interventions), and issues of conflicts of interest. An ERC needs to approve the ethical conduct of an insider researcher and give due consideration to potential harm to the population being researched – which may well be defined as 'vulnerable'. One of three outcomes is possible, depending on the ERC members' own values and their culturally informed impressions of what defines notions of vulnerability:

- this project may be regarded as low risk, seeing that the researcher is employed in the context under a professional code, that the review of practice is regarded as quality assurance, and that the project can be regarded as observational;
- it may be regarded by a university or other ERC to which the researcher may be affiliated, as requiring informed consent from the patient or their caregiver to allow data collection by a competent practitioner (not necessarily the health practitioner involved with the patient, due to conflict of interest concerns), and approval from both the manager at the hospital and at the residential care home for the project to proceed; or
- it may require consent from the patient, caregiver, the researcher's manager, and the manager at the residential care home with assurances that the employment status of any health practitioners involved in this study (assisting with the identification of potential participants) will not be affected if they choose to participate or decline to participate in this study.

The implications of such decisions for the implementation of the project are obvious. In each instance, the actions of the researchers and the expectations of the participants will be quite different. Where the project is regarded as low risk, consent will be implied through the hospital admission, and conflicts of interest avoided due the expectation of the social worker's role in the hospital. Where high risk is anticipated, levels of consent will be required by a range of individuals, and the social worker will have to carefully manage potential conflicts of interest. Either way, how the risk of harm to participants would be prevented and how good research has been supported is not clear.

Debates continue as to whether ethical review processes adequately anticipate concerns in practice at all (Shore, 2007). One of the early stages of ethical review is normally the completion of an application form for a research ethics committee. For many researchers, this is a formality, a hurdle to surmount before they can do the research. Guillemin and Gillam (2004, p. 263) warn that researchers have learned to write responses to the questions in "ethics-committee speak". This involves using language that reassures the committee that researchers are competent and experienced and can be trusted. As mentioned earlier, this may well be the place where the decisions of incompetent researchers need careful management, as not all researchers are able to fully consider risks or reassure ERCs about the ethical conduct of the research. Guillemin and Gillam regard this part of ethical conduct as "procedural ethics" and distinguish this from ethics in practice (p. 267). The latter involves "ethically important moments" in doing research – the difficult, often subtle, and usually unpredictable situations that arise in the practice of doing research and do not necessarily involve an ethical dilemma, but some kind of ethical issue nonetheless.

In a project on the experiences and needs of Black African new settlers living with HIV, ethics committee approval from three different institutions included the expectation for participants to be offered compensation in the form of a $50 voucher. In terms of procedures, the reporting of ethical risks were managed to satisfy the ERCs' requirements. However, within a couple of interviews, it became clear that some participants were in such dire financial need that they were prepared to offer their information to access the $50. The ethical dilemma for the researchers, whether or not these participants were truly voluntary or were participating only for the voucher, resulted in the participants receiving the voucher without further participation in the interview and the data collected being withdrawn. This dilemma was never discussed with the ERCs, as they had no processes in place to monitor the practice ethics. What would have been useful is a structure similar to those available to clinicians in a medical setting (more about this later), where dilemmas can be discussed with ethics consultants at an ethics forum or with professional ethicists on an as-need basis, rather than as a once-off approval before formal commencement of a project, weighed against generally conceptualised notions of risk and vulnerability. This however raises issues of resourcing and competence, which we will consider shortly.

As such, we argue that ethics committees are currently and increasingly tasked with the responsibility to manage risk, not to do good ethics or manage ethical conduct. In the process, their level of concern about the participants is unclear. This is also evident in recent developments driven by accountants and tax authorities in the interest of financial management of research funding. It is proposed that spending of research funds is monitored with the expectation that any money disseminated to research participants is to be reported against the name of that participant. This is very much implemented in the context of managing risk and transparency for the sake of the tax collector. However, we need to consider the implications for confidentiality and the ethical dilemma it poses when researchers are required to record the names of participants to their study and any compensation they may have received on a discoverable document. Such agendas are driven by external stakeholders with the main focus on accountability, which may well result in research being conducted only with people willing to be named. Researchers may well end up doing publishable research to satisfy funders and power elites, not on topics that serve the needs of communities. Naturally, there are ways to deal with this, but it is of concern that researchers need to find a way ethically to manage dilemmas that are put in place to manage risk, and not inherent to the research proper.

Strategies to advance research ethics in practice

There is a place to consider risk, but the question that needs careful consideration is who needs to manage this risk. We propose that some issues of risk can and should be monitored in practice or at least through collective deliberation, reflection, and action, or what Elwood (2007, p. 330) refers to as "participatory ethics".

Reconstructed notions of vulnerability

Ott (2014, p. 629) reminds us that the 'principle of respect for person demands protection of those more vulnerable, not exclusion [from research]'. In an attempt to ensure ethical conduct of research, the safeguard of both participants and researchers, and accountability of organisations in the conduct of research, we need to apply different strategies from those required for individualistic, agenda-driven, and outcome-guided scientific studies in order to prevent the unintentional silencing of voices. Different strategies become more pronounced for researchers utilising participatory approaches, grappling with the politics of collaboration, positionality, accountability, and responsibility, and even more so in the context of indigenous research (Smith, 2008). As has become clear throughout the chapters in this book, this requires power elites to become sensitive to notions of power relationships and to understand how vulnerability is defined and considered, but it also requires researchers to name and acknowledge these notions.

It is important to remember that ERCs are made up of researchers them-selves and most often peers of those submitting ethics applications, as well as community members who are meant to be representing 'the researched'. Managing research ethics is a joint responsibility that requires a collec-tive reconstruction of vulnerability. According to Wolf (2010), ERCs often have to draw their own conclusions about the relationship between the researcher and the participants when researchers themselves ignore or underplay the power differential. It is recommended that support for col-laborative research approaches is fostered at all levels – including with and within ERCs, so that stakeholders can share in the move from the power-in-dominance model towards a power-sharing model for complex social contexts (Wolf, 2010). This does not imply that careful consideration of aspects such as implied coercion, for instance, is not needed when service users are asked to respond to a survey about their satisfaction with the service, or where research is conducted in one's own context. However, this consideration must preferably be made on the concern for coercion, taking into account that most potential research participants do have the agency to refuse participation. Decisions should not be made exclusively for concern of the perceived vulnerability of the participant or risk to the organisation.

In essence, balanced consideration of 'risk of harm' is required. Man-agers and governance bodies understandably want to minimise risk to an organisation, and so create policies and ethical codes of conduct that minimise perceived risk and require consistent and authorised approaches to risky situations. As such, they tend to force ERCs to be overprotec-tive and make decisions about how to minimise the risk presented to the organisation (and the public). Once again, this problem-oriented approach leads to a risk-management perspective (based on problems and deficits) rather than a salutogenic or strength-based approach (Greene & Cohen, 2005), as proposed in an earlier chapter. However, to move away from consistent and authorised approaches to risk will require a consideration of and response to context for every ethics application. This poses real challenges for ERCs that are already overburdened and include members who do not have the interest or training to consider the context of some social research projects.

One solution to this dilemma is to reconstruct vulnerability from giv-ing consent to avoiding harm and the promoting of wellbeing (Schouten, 2015). As consistently highlighted in this book, critical understandings of what constitutes vulnerability are essential to address issues of vulner-ability. We argue that ERCs and researchers alike should consider that all people may be vulnerable at one point or another rather than to consider vulnerability as a characteristic of pre-determined categories of populations. Identifying persons as vulnerable can lead to increased resources or protections (Fawcett, 2009; Finlayson, 2015) but can also lead to increased social control. A reconstructed notion of vulnerability will require an interest in the people involved in research rather than an interest in risk, and challenge us to move away from definitions of risk and vulnerability and refocus on people and wellbeing.

Acknowledgement of professional ethics

Another solution is for research ethics to be considered alongside personal and professional ethics and in the context of inclusion and exclusion. Many researchers involved in professional practice are affiliated with professional bodies and guided by codes of ethics. At times, ERCs consider aspects of risk and vulnerability in research as separate to those guiding professional practice, or even as irrelevant or as a threat to research ethics. This is supported and even encouraged by authors such as Guillemin and Gillam (2004), who questioned the relevance of professional codes for actual research practice when they wrote, "In terms of usefulness in addressing ethical issues that arise in [research] practice, professional ethical codes are largely not practical or applicable and can serve only as general guidelines" (p. 263). However, we argue that it is important to inculcate ethical research conduct in the professional conduct of some professions in order to ensure that professional ethical codes are both practical and applicable for research. For professional ethics to be considered as beneficial in the conduct of research in practice, educators need to ensure that students develop critical thinking skills so that they are able to make good ethical decisions and not rely on personal values in the consideration of vulnerability, harm, informed consent, and conflicts of interest. This suggests a need for more informed engagement with ethical research.

This is also true for ethics committee members. Gambrill (2010, p. 35) refers to this as the "ethics of discretion", where professionals are given special privileges based on special knowledge and values, assumed to be transferred to them during professional education. This special education is assumed to prepare them to exercise discretion wisely in making decisions. The phrase highlights ethical obligations of various stakeholders to exercise discretion wisely and honestly for the benefits of participants and to identify when their discretion may be limited for whatever reason, including ignorance, biases, or resources. It is assumed, though, that knowledge, skills, values, and experience to determine what is best in professional practice are transferrable to other contexts, i.e., research conduct. This not to say that we can have a blanket disclaimer that all professionals working under an ethical code in practice will automatically be exemplary in their practice of research ethics. Many professionals choose to do research for ethical reasons, but doing so does not circumvent ethical dilemmas. But as with other contextual factors considered below, the profile of the researcher conducting the research should at least be a factor in considering the wellbeing of participants, rather than their protection from harm.

Participatory ethical review

Institutional rules for ethical practice in research and systematic oversight of researchers, however partial and frustrating they may be, ensure that all university-based research has at least one forum where the ethics and human impacts of its activities must be considered (Elwood, 2007, p. 337). This institutional commitment is tremendously important for all of us. As such, the solution is not to end institutional structures for ethical review. The challenge for research that really protects stakeholders of such endeavours and provides assurances for the original intent of ethical review (namely to ensure the legal and safe management of human participants in experimentation) is to reconceptualise the status, power, and responsibility of ERCs. It seems as though there is value in finding a collaborative solution to a collective problem. There is no benefit to anyone simply to criticise a committee's decisions about ethical conduct in the development of a research project, or for researchers to develop creative answers to questions by ERCs in an attempt to reassure them that the researchers are ethically competent in their conduct. The importance and complexity of ethical conduct in research place responsibility not just on ERCs, but on every single researcher, student, and educator. Ethics reviews become not box ticking exercises, but full and open-minded engagement of all stakeholders: research, ERC, participants, and communities.

Some approaches to research clearly require increased dialogue and engagement between ERCs, researchers, and research participants prior to and during the research process, in order to allow members of committees to perform more mindful reviews (Guta, Nixon, & Wilson, 2013). Elwood (2007) advocates for a truly participatory approach to research in which greater knowledge of and engagement with ERCs forms a basis for instituting more equitable and socially just research. Gilbert (2006) proposes the development of environmental health and community review boards as a supplement to the traditional ethical review processes to enable this. He envisages a committee that combines the fundamental responsibilities and ethical concepts of the traditional committees with an expanded ethical construct of dignity, veracity, sustainability, and justice in addressing the rights and concerns of the community. This seems sensible, but it is all premised on the competence, values, resourcing, and culturally informed impressions of the ERC members. Over and above the fact that ERC members traditionally operate within a biomedical framework, limited resourcing restricts their ability to develop a knowledge base of different research methodologies and contexts (Guta,Nixon, & Wilson, 2013). This challenge is compounded by the life experience, culture, or customs of committee members that often do not adequately reflect diverse values, skills, and understanding of different and complex contexts or population groups, including indigenous, tribal, or collectivist cultures as highlighted by Smith (2008).

As such, the solution seems to be somewhere in the middle – in the nexus of researchers, ethical committee members, and research participants. We propose a process of peer discussion and deliberation on ethically challenging aspects to which none of us have simple answers, but where we can proceed carefully and in ways we can defend to our peers and those affected by our decisions if called upon to do so. This will be a more modest role than that of ERC membership, but in our view, a more valuable role. This proposition will sound very familiar and resonate strongly with clinicians who have access to Clinical Ethics Advisory Groups (CEAGs). Dare (2010) finds that CEAGs aim to provide a forum in which practitioners can raise ethical problems and check their own judgments and intuitions, while benefitting from open discussion with other clinicians and appropriate outsiders. More importantly, CEAGs and their members contribute to this process by advising and supplementing, not replacing, the judgment of clinicians. This proposal assumes that membership of such advisory groups includes awareness and representation of cultural diversity, ethical and legal expertise, and current and advanced expertise in the area under consideration.

Scheman calls for an ethics of epistemology, "a norm of epistemic sustainability: research methods and practices that cultivate, rather than undermine, the ground on which especially less privileged others can successfully pursue knowledge, meeting their epistemic needs as they define them" (2014, p. 169). With collaborative ethics advisory groups, we may eventually be able to achieve such an ethics of epistemology, as discussion and deliberation on ethically challenging topics will be inclusive of those affected by the decisions and be a learning and empowering process for all involved. Implementation will not be without its own challenges – but then, no ethical conduct will ever be.

Key questions for Chapter 8

This chapter considers the importance of ethics review panels in the ways research with so-called vulnerable and marginalised communities is carried out. These panels can be so concerned about 'protecting' these communities that the voices of these communities may not be heard. We have proposed that a way for ethic panels to manage this perceived risk is to encourage researchers to engage more, rather than less, with such persons and communities.

- Do you think ethics committees have an important role to play in the ethical conduct of research? Why?
- What in your view are the elements that should impact a decision of 'risk of harm'?
- What do you regard as 'voluntary and informed consent' for the purposes of research?
- Do you have a dual role as researcher and professional? Do you find the ethical requirements for your professional conduct in conflict with your research conduct? Why?
- To what extent should people affected by research be allowed to shape ethical review committees' agendas?

---

9 Re-imagining vulnerability and marginality

Assessing the claims

One of the implicit aims of this book has been to encourage readers, service providers, service funders, and service users to stop and reflect before using the familiar and popular terms vulnerability and marginality. These terms are very much in 21st century professional and political discourse in many countries, and if we have done nothing else with this book, we hope at least to have encouraged thoughtful use of these words. We hope, of course, to do more than merely encourage reflection. We hope that we will encourage readers to re-imagine what these terms may mean, to interrogate the values that underpin them, and to reconceptualise the delivery of services to communities and populations who have been forced to the margins, or who have been constructed and labelled as powerless in their states and societies.

We began this exploration by investigating and critiquing accepted concepts of vulnerability and marginality. These concepts emerged in their present form largely in notionally capitalist societies that believe that wealth is good and the good have wealth, and where neoliberal economic theory has dominated since the late 1970s. In these societies, social inequalities have resulted from neoliberal economic policy, to the extent that this inequality has been called "one of, if not the most important political issue" of our time (Martin, 2016). Concepts of vulnerability and marginality have achieved currency because they have either deliberately, or as an unexpected consequence (depending on how Machiavellian your political beliefs are), been endorsed by states that now are faced with responding to or managing so-called vulnerable and marginalised persons. We have considered these concepts that have been actualised legally and popularly through the lens of sexuality and intimacy. Since the global financial crisis of 2007–08, the centre of gravity of the intellectual debate about neoliberal economics and unfettered capitalism has shifted (Martin, 2016), and free-market capitalists and monetarists are now being challenged even by economists who were previously strong advocates of neoliberal economic theory.

Because we write from a social work perspective, we are compelled to explore these ideas not merely as theory, but also in social practice and research. The shift in thinking about neoliberal economic policies creates a space for social and health policy-makers, practitioners, and researchers to challenge the implications of these notions in policy, care delivery, and in setting out research agendas. We have argued that traditional top-down care and policy has promoted managerial protocols and care plans that are largely organisationally based and driven by fiscal efficiencies and the management of risk to the organisation rather than by the needs of the person. Such top-down models have been adopted by care delivery agencies, even while caregivers in those agencies advocate for person-centred care models. By rejecting essentialised notions of vulnerability and marginality, we have proposed an alternative care paradigm that is driven by the needs of the individual service user, client, or resident. This shift in emphasis is consistent with the growing body of literature highlighting individuals becoming active participants in their care, rather than passive consumers of services (Pols et al., 2009; Wilkinson & Whitehead, 2009). We have recognised that approaches such as person-centred care are not novel, but have been in place for decades. However, we have also recognised that what passes for person-centred practice is often something different, and that in practice, truly person-centred care is neither possible nor practical. Instead, we recognise that negotiated care is the more likely alternative to managerial care. We recognise that individualised models of care in any form may be initially resource-intensive; therefore, we, along with all stakeholders, must ask whether such models can be shown to be both effective and efficient in the long term.

In this concluding chapter, then, we will raise two questions. First, how is the reader to evaluate the feasibility of the claims we have made throughout this book? We will suggest that before our claims can be assessed, the reader will need first to critique traditional approaches to evaluation that are largely based on neoliberal values and exclusively positivist notions of evaluation that valorise particular kinds of knowledge. If we have been at all persuasive, the reader will then not only evaluate our claims in a non-traditional way, but then go on to critique the approach to evaluation of all kinds of social services and health care delivery. Second, how can these reconceptualised services themselves be evaluated? The answer to this question is the same: by critiquing traditional positivist notions of knowledge and by moving beyond neoliberal notions of risk, managerialism, and accountability. Because every situation, discipline, and jurisdiction will be different in terms of objectives, models of evaluation, and accountability, we will keep our discussion at a relatively theoretical level, inviting readers to consider and critique their assumptions of current and traditional approaches in their own contexts.

Critiquing 'outputs'

In the neoliberal context, social service agencies are under pressure from governments, funders, and other external stakeholders to provide evidence of what is measurably produced or done (outputs) rather than what is achieved (outcomes). Part of this pressure derives from funding models that are underpinned by positivist assumptions that are more easily relayed to the public and its legislatures through the use of numbers and statistics than by telling complex stories that take more than a few moments of a sound bite. The service data collected on a regular basis by most agencies can demonstrate outputs much more easily than outcomes: the number of clients served; the number of people participating in programmes; the range of professional interventions on offer; media stories generated; stakeholder meetings coordinated; grant applications made and received; business relations developed; trainings delivered. These outputs are easier to collect and interpret than outcomes. Outcomes include improvement in clients' wellbeing; the value of integrated services; the community impact of a programme; the effect of a policy on the delivery of services; and the perceived value of a service for family members or communities of users. Measuring outputs is a reasonably straightforward kind of counting, which can then be married up with the overall cost of a service to develop a kind of rude efficiency measure: what is the cost per unit output. Efficiency has become a primary driver of programme evaluation not only because it responds to demands for accountability to funders and taxpayers ("Eliminate waste!"), but because it is also easier for practitioners and managers of agencies who must report to funders in order to receive another round of resources. (In the early days of the HIV epidemic, one of your authors recalls having to count pamphlets distributed as a measure of health education programme effectiveness. Only much later did things like measuring client knowledge or behaviour change come into play.)

Outcome information by its very nature is complex and messy. Outcomes are influenced by factors such as individual client characteristics and variables, related interventions, programmes and players within and outside of the agency, as well as by social, economic, and environmental factors. Outcomes involve qualitative as well as quantitative measures and frequently are more approximate than exact, particularly in the social services sector. In addition, such models must be sufficiently flexible to accommodate varying levels of progress towards achieving an 'outcome': while the goal of a literacy programme is to encourage a participant to read an entire book, a successful outcome for some clients may be simply to sound out the chapter titles, or even to learn a few words. By some traditional measures, if the participant fails to read the entire book, then the outcome will not have been met, while in reality, sounding out chapter titles, or even arriving at the programme venue on time, will be a significant indicator not only of participation or engagement but also of progress towards the goal. This approach would be particularly significant in sexual health harm reduction programmes that encourage condom use: if a client who did not previously use condoms uses them 10 percent of the time, this must be considered progress, even though it is unlikely to be 100 percent effective. Some agencies still measure their success by the number of condoms they distribute in order to prevention transmission of HIV and other sexually transmitted infections. Yet in jurisdictions where sex work is illegal, possession of condoms is considered presumptive evidence of illegal behaviour (Open Society Foundations, 2012), and paradoxically, sex workers risk arrest simply by carrying the condoms they have been given by government-funded programmes to protect them. Success for these health education programmes, then, was measured by how many sex workers they can convince to carry and use condoms even when that put them at risk for arrest and prosecution. Health educators consequently did not meet the target number of condoms distributed not because they were not working hard to do so, or because the clients were not interested in reducing their risks, but because of a legal environment the government itself had created. The complexity of this situation is an example of how difficult it can be to capture outcome data using traditional accountability models.

We are not proposing that social and human services abandon accountability, as funds are always limited for one reason or another, and funding should be allocated to programmes that are both efficient and that 'work' (that is, are effective). We are proposing that human service funders and providers move beyond merely positivist notions of accountability and rebalance assessments of efficiency and efficacy, so that efficiency is seen in the context of the effectiveness of negotiated care. We will explore this further below.

As we said earlier, we are intentionally keeping this discussion at a relatively theoretical level because we are mindful that much of how pro-grammes are resourced and assessed varies considerably by governments both by country and/or state, and historically within the same jurisdic-tion over time. Meaningful social development, however, can only come about if there is the political will and, coincident with that will, popular support. If governments continue to remain focussed on managing risk, or measuring success by outputs, for instance, then the wellbeing of cli-ents, residents, or patients will always remain secondary to accountability for funds. Wellbeing, as we have seen, is much more difficult to measure than 'safety' or avoiding risk. Professionals, legislators, service users, and the public will need to be educated about what constitutes efficiency and efficacy in the social services sector. The popular media in particular will need to be educated to look beyond the story of the day and critically take a long view of social change, the appropriate use of public resources, and how this is reported.

Assessing services and care

The purpose of an evaluation can be three-fold, aimed at: gathering infor-mation for improving the design, development, formation, and implemen-tation of a programme (formative evaluation); describing the process of a programme as it is being developed (process evaluation); or assessing the impact, outcome, or worth of a programme (summative evaluation) (Fou-ché, 2015). Summative evaluation is mostly aimed at measuring effective-ness (impact and outcome evaluation) and efficiency. The current outcomes approach to the provision of social services considerably shifts the focus of social services as meeting community needs: governments now deter-mine needs, and funding is aligned with government priorities rather than defined by needs identified by social services agencies, users, and/or the community (O'Brien, 2016). Outcomes-based funding therefore becomes the key to shaping public social spending and priorities. When outcomes-based funding is aligned with a particular understanding of vulnerability, the implications are clear: social service agencies deliver services that are funded by the government to communities that fit government definitions of vulnerability, and are based on evidence of outcomes achieved accord-ing to measures determined by the government. Because government pri-orities are often shaped by political expedience and always with the next election in mind, it is not surprising that non-prioritised needs, even when there is robust advocacy, remain unconsidered and unfunded.

It is within this context that we can turn our attention to efficiency and effectiveness in assessing social and health care.

Assessing efficiency

Efficiency assessments are not at all common in social service delivery, partly due to the fact that the question of costs really only becomes crucial when the effectiveness of a programme has been determined. Moreover, for some agencies, efficiency is really only pertinent when the continuation of the programme is considered in comparison with other programmes designed to affect similar outcomes. As such, efficiency becomes crucial at the funding application level – particularly when outcomes-based funding is the key to spending. The crucial factor, then, is what measures are considered in assessing cost efficiency. Naturally, immediate costs include facilities, staffing, resources, and overhead. But additional costs may include those more difficult to measure: family costs of time spent away from home, the cost of workdays lost in order to provide care for a dependent at home, or the emotional distress of managing complex systems. Efficiencies can also be assessed in services avoided or not needed: trips to the emergency department not taken, falls that did not happen, laboratory tests that are not required, medications that are not needed, domestic violence incidents that did not happen, children who did not run away. These 'absent' measures are far more difficult to assess, however, especially on an individual basis. An agency may have the opportunity to track care that is not necessary on a year-on-year basis to assess the positive efficiencies of changes in service.

If residents with dementia can be in charge of their own lives, then notions of vulnerability must be revisited. They will no longer be resigned to chairs in the day room, but supported to garden, be active, cook and clean, or to socialise as ways of challenging traditional notions of vulnerability. In doing so, they no longer need to be marginalised, but supported to maximise their autonomy, their relationships, and their engagement with their environments. This kind of care is emerging in models around the world. By exploring these measures in their own settings, readers can assess whether person-centred or negotiated models of care are efficacious and effective. We then generalise from residential care for dementia to other residential care, and finally to other so-called vulnerable groups, and suggest ways in which services to these other groups can be reconceptualised. We propose that efficiency should be reconceptualised as a factor, but not the determining factor of assessing care.

Assessing effectiveness

Closely linked to neoliberal polemics related to outcomes are debates on measures of effectiveness. The expectation for effectiveness is nothing new and has featured in debates in social work since the early 1970s. A seminal article by Fischer (1973) entitled 'Is casework effective?' began the debate with the disturbing finding that the condition of 50 percent of clients who receive casework services deteriorated. In the two decades subsequent to this paper, a number of studies were reported and debates published on 'what works', convincing the profession that indeed social casework is effective. One of these claimed that the principles of quality practice include the clients' experience of the intervention (Wood, 1978). This introduced an important direction in the development of the debates on effectiveness of social work by valuing the client experience. Client satisfaction may be a very good measure of the extent to which practitioners have made a difference. However, in considering the range, scope, and extent of resources needed to enable such satisfaction, we need to contemplate levels of need – which is directly linked to the notion of person-centred care. In negotiated care, client self-determination or self-efficacy might be more accurate measures of effectiveness than client satisfaction.

A number of frameworks are promoted internationally in the social services sectors to facilitate the complex discussions related to outcomes, with the Results Based Accountability (RBA) framework currently one of the most popular. It is one model, among many current and historical frameworks, that accommodates neoliberal approaches of accountability. RBA was developed by Friedman (2005), author of the book *Trying Hard Is Not Good Enough*. One of the reasons for RBA's popularity is that it has encouraged the measurement of accountability at both population level and programme or service level. This framework makes it explicit that outcomes can be developed and assessed at the national, regional, community, agency, or programme level. It encourages multiple sectors to working together towards collective impact. Yet the RBA still sits within a framework that works from neoliberal and positivist approaches because it remains primarily focussed on money and requires agencies to report against how they use money rather than encouraging them to balance resource considerations with person-centred care models and client outcomes.

This RBA approach has had currency internationally. For instance, New Zealand's Ministry of Social Development (MSD) introduced an 'Investing in Services for Outcomes' (ISO) approach aimed at improving outcomes for families and communities by implementing, amongst other things, an organisational capability framework (Ministry of Social Development, n.d.). There are two core aspects related to this development that may resonate with models used elsewhere: first, this approach emphasises that no single organisation can be solely responsible for addressing complex social issues. Large-scale social development will come from improving cross-sector coordination and sharing a collective vision, rather than isolated interventions from individual organisations. And second, it acknowledges that organisational capability is essential to achieving an outcomes approach. The calls for more enhanced and effective partnerships and models of 'integrated care' are intensifying internationally and increasingly seen as the norm, rather than the exception. In the UK, collaborative work has in recent years moved from being an optional extra of public service practice to being a core competency for individuals and teams (Dickson & O'Flynn, 2016). Moving from these policy directives to practice is another matter altogether, but it is significant to see partnerships acknowledged as core business by governments and policy-makers. It remains unclear if this has led to better outcomes for people who use services or even how to measure those outcomes if they exist. Several projects question whether joint commissioning, integrated care among compartmentalised stakeholders, and the involvement of families and communities increase, decrease, or have no impact on the quality, effectiveness, and costs of care (see, for example, Dickinson et al., 2012).

One of the things that follow from the integrated accountability models is that evaluators will need to reconsider the concept of 'client' as the unit of evaluation. Clients may not only be individuals, of course; the concept of client can include families of origin (blood kin) and families of choice, neighbourhoods and communities, organisations and agencies; they may be one or more of these and in various combinations. How, for instance, can we assess the impact of negotiated care on the family of a woman with advanced dementia living in residential care? That the adult children of the woman can continue to care for their own families, go to work or school, maintain an income and pay their taxes are all indirect benefits to the residential care the resident receives. If the woman had to live with one of her adult children, it is likely that none of these other things would be possible; yet these additional dimensions are difficult to measure and record on a monthly report. Assessment models of both efficiency and effectiveness must interrogate and develop the notion of client. The only way we can more accurately assess a person-centred or negotiated care model, or a service responding to a reconceptualised paradigm of vulnerability, is to find a way to capture the intangible humanistic values, including compassion and partnership, and the prevention of negative outcomes. Positivist methodologies are not very good at this. The real challenge is not necessarily in what we assess, but in the values we assess, who assesses, and how we understand aspects of practice that will indicate what we consider effectiveness.

Conclusion

We suggested at the outset of this chapter that it was important to provide a way to assess the claims we have made in this book. What we have suggested is that the ways vulnerability and marginality have been conceptualised by neoliberal governments have penetrated not only the metrics but also the methods that we use to assess human services in the 21st century. We have suggested that the ways human services and programmes in neoliberal environments are evaluated must themselves be critiqued. Notions of risk, managerialism, and accountability rely on *outputs*, or measures of activity and production. Instead, we have proposed that we must increasingly develop assessment models that measure and demonstrate *outcomes* in clients. Furthermore, we have proposed that the science of evaluation must be enhanced: approaches to evaluation that are based exclusively on positivist notions of evaluation that valorise particular kinds of knowledge must be broadened to include a range of less quantifiable metrics. We have not suggested that human services programmes should not be accountable: indeed, because many of these programmes rely on public funding, however limited, accountability for funds and how funding is used is an important part of programme assessment. But human lives are complex and messy, and not easily predicted or managed. But surely it is time to recall that the point of human services is to enhance and support the lives of humans: not balance sheets, risk management, or poll results.

We recognise very well that reconceptualising human services evaluation in these ways, and challenging the dominant scientific paradigm of positivism, with its emphasis on statistical reporting, will take great courage and political will. It will require re-educating politicians, funders, programme managers, human service professionals, client, residents, and patients. It will require innovative thinking on the part of researchers, ethicists, and academics. Because this is the case, we believe it is time to get started.

Key questions for Chapter 9

This chapter invites you to assess the claims set out in this book. It also invites you critically to evaluate the ways you assess these claims. The paradigm of positivist science – that is, quantitative research that claims to be objective and empirical – is held up as the preferred standard of measurement, and is frequently used by funders to evaluate social care and human services. We have suggested that positivist approaches are neither adequate nor as objective as they claim, and that by relying solely on these approaches, we may miss very important parts of the evaluation story. The implications of reconceptualising vulnerability and marginality, then, are that the very ways these concepts are measured and described must themselves be reconsidered.

- How do you evaluate the impact of the work you do? Who is the 'audience' for your evaluation? Do you think the evaluations you carry out on your work represent accurately the full impact of what you do?
- Do you mainly consider an outcomes or output kind of evaluation in the work you do? Are these evaluations driven by funding, compliance, or programmatic requirements? If you could design an ideal evaluation for the kind of work that you do, what would it look like?
- How feasible do you consider the reconceptualisations of vulnerability and marginality proposed in this book in the delivery of social services? What can you do to influence the feasibility?

Restoring the human

The purpose of this book has been to explore vulnerability and marginality as they intersect with power and privilege. We explored these concepts through the lenses of intimacy and sexuality, the deepest and most personal places in our lives, places that require personal risk and honesty. We have proposed that the words vulnerability and marginality are used by people in power to name and control groups of people, and are complex and created. We have suggested that an appropriate response to the concepts of vulnerability and marginality is not merely to 'help' vulnerable and marginalised individuals and communities, but to critique those with power who create and label those individuals and communities. A key message from this book is that it is important for social and health care workers, clinicians, and other professionals to understand the social, political, and economic contexts in which they are working because those contexts inevitably shape not only the work, but the way we understand and construct our clients. We have proposed that it is a task of helping professionals not merely to 'help', but to consider critically their philosophical frameworks, epistemologies, and ethical underpinnings in order to avoid replicating and reproducing power and privilege in their work. Contemporary social work, for instance, can extend itself beyond its statist top-down heuristic to a model where theory, agency, worker, and client are co-creators in the development of understandings of theory, practice, and evaluation. This heuristic is not static, but dynamic, and informed by the social, political, economic, and intellectual environments from which they emerge.

For human service professionals, educators, and researchers to work critically and authentically will require them to be reflexive and self-aware, as well as to engage critically with the epistemological frameworks that the helping professions have inherited. But this critical engagement provides a way forward that challenges notions of power, privilege, and labelling of clients as vulnerable and marginalised, and thereby to control them. This kind of engagement may help individuals, groups, and societies into more authentic understandings of self and of social cohesion.

We have proposed that the relationships between resident and caregiver, medical staff and patient, or worker and client have been shaped by concepts of vulnerability and marginality that established power relationships that are replicated throughout the human services sectors. The construction of these kinds of relationships has led to an approach that focuses on risk rather than residents. An alternative to this kind of relationship recognises the strengths and resilience of individuals and communities, rather than their perceived or constructed vulnerabilities. We have advocated for ensuring that human beings are at the centre of human services. Person-centred and negotiated care approaches increase autonomy and self-determination, and return to persons the authorship of their own lives. Person-centred care can apply not only to health and mental health care, but also to public policy and funding: such approaches do not problematise individuals but encourage their resilience by building on individual and community strengths. Such care models will also require a philosophical and policy shift by neoliberal governments, which have capitalised on vulnerability in order to control populations under the banner of managing risk and saving taxpayer money. A shift to person-centred care would capitalise on resilience and foster autonomy, rather than focus on control and compliance.

We have also considered the way power relationships that develop from the labels of vulnerability and marginality impact social research. This influence includes not only the topics that are chosen to be researched, but also relationships between researcher and participants. We have encouraged collective approaches to research, and increased levels of engagement with groups of people who are invested in the outcome of the research: this kind of collectivist approach to research will result in greater inclusion and protection of individuals and communities. Participatory research designs must extend to research ethics: in the interest of protecting labelled vulnerable and marginalised groups, much valuable research is never begun. Ethics panels and committees must be supported to find ways beyond a relatively superficial risk-management approach in order to reconsider how they understand so-called vulnerable persons and communities. This will also require an epistemological shift to a more inclusive approach to research ethics.

Finally, we have proposed that our claims must be assessed in local contexts, but that current assessment methods themselves have been significantly influenced by neoliberal values and methods. We have encouraged critiquing those methods so that we can look not only at efficiency and value for money, but also at outcomes that re-assess what 'value' means in the lives of individuals and communities. Once human services professionals, researchers, and educators begin to unravel concepts of vulnerability and marginality, a number of important questions emerge, and we find ourselves questioning the entire foundation on which our social care structures have been constructed. This, in our view, is a good thing. The domination of social care by business and efficiency models has resulted in a kind of theoretical torpor that accepts these models as unavoidable and inescapable as overburdened agency staff struggle to keep up with increasing demand with fewer resources. It is our hope to have added our voices to the calls for new critical paradigms that return human beings to the centre of social care and human services. It is not only possible, it is necessary – and it is time.

Key concluding questions for this book

- What do you think have been the key impacts of government economic policies on the work that you do?
- How do you evaluate the claims of this book?
- Based on the proposal that we need to reconceptualise vulnerability and marginality, what changes, if any, will you make in the ways you relate to funders, contract managers, and agency managers?
- How might you evaluate the claim that human beings have been displaced by economic philosophy and political expediency in social care and human services?
- How will these ideas influence the ways you work with clients? With colleagues?
- How will these ideas shape your decisions about your professional future?

References

Aday, L. A. (2011). *At risk in America: The health and health care needs of vulnerable populations in the United States*. San Francisco, CA: Jossey-Bass.

Adger, W. N. (2006). Vulnerability. *Global Environmental Change, 16*, 268–281. doi:10.1016/j.gloenvcha.2006.02.006

Adjovi, L. (2016). *Gregoire Ahongbong: Freeing people chained for being ill*. Retrieved from www.bbc.com/news/magazine-35586177

Aldrich, R. (2003). *Colonialism and homosexuality*. London: Routledge.

Arbodela, G. M., & Murray, S. O. (1985). The dangers of lexical inference with special reference to Maori homosexuality. *Journal of Homosexuality, 12*(1), 129–134.

Armstrong, R. (2010). Fairness and equity in the provision of anti-retroviral therapy: Some reflections from Lesotho. *Developing World Bioethics, 10*(3), 129–140. doi:10.1111/j.1471–8847–2009.00267.x

Bamford, R. (2014). Ethical review of health systems research: Vulnerability and the need for philosophy in research ethics. *American Journal of Bioethics, 14*(2), 38–39.

Basic Income Earth Network (n.d.). *History of basic income*. Retrieved from http://basicincome.org/basic-income/history

Bauer, M., Fetherstonhaugh, D., Tarzia, L., Nay, R., Wellman, D., & Beattie, E. (2013). 'I always look under the bed for a man'. Needs and barriers to the expression of sexuality in residential aged care: The views of residents with and without dementia. *Psychology and Sexuality, 4*(3), 296–309. doi:10.1136/bmj.c810

Bauer, M., McAuliffe, L., Nay, R., & Chenco, C. (2013). Sexuality in older adults: Effect of an education intervention on attitudes and beliefs of residential aged care staff. *Educational Gerontology, 39*(2), 82–91. doi:10.1080/03601277.2012.682953

BBC News. (2016a). *PCC Sue Mountsevens says putting mentally ill in cells 'Dickensian'*. Retrieved from www.bbc.com/news/uk-england-bristol-35580191

BBC News. (2016b). *US to end federal use of private prisons*. Retrieved from www.bbc.com/news/world-us-canada-37124183

Beck, U. (2009). *World at risk*. Cambridge, UK: Polity Press.

Becker, G. J. (2005). Human subjects investigation: Timeless lessons of Nuremberg and Tuskegee. *Journal of American College of Radiology, 2*, 215–217. doi:10.1016/j.jacr.2004.11.018

Becksted, A. L. (2012). Can we change sexual orientation. *Archives of Sexual Behavior, 41*, 121–134. doi:10.1007/s10508–012–9922-x

Beemyn, B., & Eliason, M. (1996). *Queer studies: A lesbian, gay, bisexual and transgender anthology*. New York, NY: NYU Press.

Belluck, P. (2015, April 14). Sex, dementia and a husband on trial at age 78. *New York Times*. Retrieved from www.nytimes.com/2015/04/14/health/sex-dementia-and-a-husband-henry-rayhons-on-trial-at-age-78.html?_r=0

Benbow, S. M., & Beeston, D. (2012). Sexuality, aging and dementia. *International Psychogeriatrics, 24*(7), 1026–1033. doi:10.1017/S1041610212000257

Bennett, B. (2015). "Stop deploying your white privilege on me!" Aboriginal and Torres Strait Islander engagement with the Australian Association of Social Workers. *Australian Social Work, 68*(1), 19–31. doi:10.1080/0312407X.2013.840325

Beresford, P., & Carr, S. (2012). *Social care, service users and user involvement*. London, UK: Jessica Kingsley.

Bergeson, S. C., & Dean, J. D. (2006). A systems approach to patient-centered care. *Journal of the American Medical Association, 296*(23), 2848–2851.

Berkin, C. R., Pinch, J. L., & Appel, C. S. (2005). *Exploring women's studies: Looking forward, looking back*. Upper Saddle River, NJ: Pearson Prentice Hall.

Blackwood, E., & Wieringa, S. E. (Eds.). (1999). *Female desires: Same-sex relations and transgender practices across cultures*. New York: Columbia University Press.

Blank, H. (2012). *Straight: The surprisingly short history of heterosexuality*. Boston, MA: Beacon Press.

Boellstorff, T. (2005). Between religion and desire: Being Muslim and gay in Indonesia [Electronic version]. *American Anthropologist, 107*(4), 575–585.

Boswell, J. (1995). *The marriage of likeness: Same-sex unions in pre-modern Europe*. London: Fontana Press.

Bradley, M. (2007). Silenced for their own protection: How the IRB marginalizes those it feigns to protect. *ACME: An International E-Journal for Critical Geographies, 6*(3), 339–349. doi:10.1.1.537.835

Braun, J. von, & Gatzweiler, F. W. (Eds.) (2014). *Marginality: Addressing the nexus of poverty, exclusion and ecology*. Dordrecht, Germany: SpringerOpen.

Bray, P., & McLean, L. (Eds.). (2015). *At the crossroads of crisis and opportunity: Interdisciplinary conversations*. Oxford, UK: Inter-Disciplinary Press.

Brewer, C. (2005). Baylan, asog, transvestism, and sodomy: Gender, sexuality and the sacred in early colonial Philippines. *Intersections* (2). Retrieved from http://intersections.anu.edu.au/issue2/carolyn2.html

Bridges, T. (2014). A very "gay" straight?: Hybrid masculinities, sexual aesthetics, and the changing relationship between masculinity and homophobia. *Gender and Society, 28*(1), 58–82. doi:10.1177/0891243213503901

Broadband Commission for Digital Development. (2015). *The state of broadband 2015*. Geneva, Switzerland. Retrieved from www.broadbandcommission.org/Documents/reports/bb-annualreport2015.pdf

Brown, K. (2014). Questioning the vulnerability zeitgeist: Care and control practices with "vulnerable" young people. *Social Policy and Society, 13*, 371–387. doi:10.1017/S1474746413000535

Buber, M. (1923/1937). *I and thou*. New York, NY: Charles Scribner & Sons.

Butler, S. S. (2004). Gay, Lesbian, Bisexual, and Transgender (GLBT) elders: The challenges and resilience of this marginalized group. *Journal of Human Behavior in the Social Environment, 9*(4), 25–44.

Buttram, M. E., Surratt, H. L., & Kurtz, S. P. (2014). Risk and protective factors associated with personal mastery among sexual minority African-American female sex workers. *Journal of Gay & Lesbian Social Services, 26*(4), 407–425. doi:10.1080/10538720.2014.956242

Cahalane, C. (2014). *Social impact bonds: Is the dream over?* Retrieved from www.theguardian.com/voluntary-sector-network/2014/may/01/social-impact-bonds-funding-model-sibs-future

Callahan, D. (2000). The vulnerability of the human condition. In P. Kemp, K. Rendtorff, & N. M. Johansen (Eds.), *Bioethics and biolaw: Four ethical principles* (pp. 115–122). Copenhagen: Rhodos International.

Campbell, P. (2001). The role of users of psychiatric services in service development – influence not power. *Psychiatric Bulletin, 25*, 87–88.

Case, K. A., Hensley, R., & Anderson, A. (2014). Reflecting on heterosexual and male privilege: Interventions to raise awareness. *Journal of Social Issues, 70*(4), 722–740. doi:10.1111/josi.12088

Cass, V. C. (1979). Homosexual identity formation: Theoretical model. *Journal of Homosexuality, 4*(3), 219–235.

Castro Varela, M. D. M., Dhawan, N., & Engel, A. (Eds.). (2011). *Hegemony and heteronormativity: Revisiting 'the political' in queer politics*. Surrey, UK: Ashgate.

Centre for Bhutan Studies & GNH Research. (2015). *Bhutan's 2015 gross national happiness index*. Retrieved from www.grossnationalhappiness.com/

Chak, A. (2015). Beyond 'he' and 'she': The rise of non-binary pronouns. *BBC News*. Retrieved from www.bbc.com/news/magazine-34901704

Chopra, D., Williams, P., & Bhaskar, V. (2011). Politics of citizenship: Experiencing state – society relations from the margins. *Contemporary South Asia, 19*(3), 243–247. doi:10.1080/09584935.2011.596275

Chou, W.-S. (2000). *Tongzhi: Politics of same-sex eroticism in Chinese societies*. New York: Haworth Press.

Cocker, C., & Hafford-Letchfield, T. (2010). Out and proud? Social work's relationship with lesbian and gay equality. *British Journal of Social Work, 40*(6), 1996–2008. doi:10.1093/bjsw/bcp158

Cohn, M. A., Fredrickson, B. L., Brown, S. L., Mikels, J. A., & Conway, A. M. (2009). Happiness unpacked: Positive emotions increase life satisfaction by building resilience. *Emotion, 9*(3), 361–368. doi:10.1037/a0015952

Cole, J. (2014). Intimacy; views from impairment and neuroscience. *Emotion, Space and Society*, *13*, 87–94. doi:http://dx.doi.org/10.1016/j.emospa.2014.01.001

Commonwealth Heads of Government. (2012). *Commonwealth charter*. London, UK. Retrieved from http://thecommonwealth.org/sites/default/files/page/documents/CharteroftheCommonwealth.pdf

Corby, B. (2006). *Applying research in social work practice*. London, UK: Open University Press.

Cornwall, S. (2010). *Sex and uncertainty in the body of Christ: Intersex conditions and Christian theology*. London: Equinox.

Cosis Brown, H., & Cocker, C. (2011). *Social work with lesbians and gay men*. London: Sage.

Council for International Organizations of Medical Sciences. (1982, 1993, 2002). *International ethical guidelines for biomedical research involving human subjects*. Geneva, Switzerland: Author.

Crompton, L. (2003). *Homosexuality and civilization*. Cambridge, MA: Harvard University Press.

Cuigini, M. (2015). Successfully navigating the human subjects approval process. *American Dental Hygienists Association*, *89*(suppl. 1), 54–56.

Cunha, D. (2014). *Why drug testing welfare recipients is a waste of taxpayer money*. Retrieved from http://time.com/3117361/welfare-recipients-drug-testing/

Dare, T. (2010). Clinical ethics committees. *Health Research Council Ethics Notes*. Retrieved from www.adhb.govt.nz/ceag/articles/Ethics%20Notes%20-%20August%20201038.pdf

DeLamater, J. D., & Hyde, J. S. (1998). Essentialism vs. social constructionism in the study of human sexuality. *Journal of Sex Research*, *35*, 10–18.

Delor, F., & Hubert, M. (2000). Revisiting the concept of "vulnerability". *Social Science & Medicine*, *50*(11), 1557–1570. doi:10.1016/S0277–9536(99)00465–7

Department for Business Innovation & Skills and Export Control Organisation. (2012). *Guidance for exporters on the various areas of export control legislation, including international regimes and treaties*. Retrieved from www.gov.uk/guidance/overview-of-export-control-legislation

Dessel, R., & Ramirez, M. (1995/2013). *Policies and procedures concerning sexual expression at the Hebrew Home at Riverdale*. Retrieved from http://ltcombudsman.org/uploads/files/issues/Sexual_Expression_PP-Hebrew_Home.pdf

Deveson, A. (2003). *Resilience*. Crows Nest, NSW: Allen & Unwin.

Dey, R. M., De Vries, M. J. W., & Bosnic-Anticevich, S. (2011). Collaboration in chronic care: Unpacking the relationship of pharmacists and general medical practitioners in primary care. *International Journal of Pharmacy Practice*, *19*(1), 21–29. doi:10.1111/j.2042–7174.2010.00070.x

Diamond, L. M. (2003a). Was it a phase? Young women's relinquishment of lesbian/bisexual identities over a 5-year period. *Journal of Personality and Social Psychology*, *84*(2), 352–364.

Diamond, L. M. (2003b). What does sexual orientation orient? A biobehavioral model distinguishing romantic love and sexual desire. *Psychological Review*, *110*(1), 173–192.

Diamond, L. M. (2006). What we got wrong about sexual identity development: Unexpected findings from a longitudinal study of young women. In A. M. Omoto & H. S. Kurtzman (Eds.), *Sexual orientation and mental health* (pp. 73–94). Washington, DC: American Psychological Association.

Dickinson, H., Glasby, J., Nicholds, A., Jeffares, S., Robinson, S., & Sullivan, H. (2012). *An exploration of definitions, processes, services and outcomes: Final report.* Southampton, UK: National Institute for Health Research.

Dickinson, H., & O'Flynn, J. (2016). *Evaluating outcomes in health and social care.* Bristol, UK: Policy Press.

Di Napoli, E. A., Breland, G. L., & Allen, R. S. (2013). Staff knowledge and perceptions of sexuality and dementia of older adults in nursing homes. *Journal of Aging and Health, 25*(7), 1087–1105. doi:10.1177/0898264313494802

Dolan, M. (2014). *The world's richest people are sitting on gigantic piles of cash that aren't earning them anything.* Retrieved from http://business.financialpost. com/news/economy/the-worlds-richest-people-are-sitting-on-gigantic-piles-of-cash-that-arent-earning-them-anything

Dubos, R. (1978). Health and creative adaptation. *Human Nature, 1,* 74–82.

Dunk-West, P., & Hafford-Letchfield, T. (Eds.). (2011). *Sexual identities and sexuality in social work.* Surrey, UK: Ashgate.

Eden Alternative®. (n.d.). *Eden Alternative®.* Retrieved from www.edenalt.org/

Ehrenfeld, M., Bronner, G., Tabak, N., Alpert, R., & Bergman, R. (1999). Sexuality among institutionalized elderly patients with dementia. *Nursing Ethics, 6*(2), 144–149.

Elias, J., & Ryan, A. (2011). A review and commentary on the factors that influence expressions of sexuality by older people in care homes. *Journal of Clinical Nursing, 20*(11–12), 1668–1676. doi:10.111/j.1365–2702.2010.06409

Eliason, M. J. (1996). Identity formation for lesbian, bisexual and gay persons: Beyond a "minoritizing" view. *Journal of Homosexuality, 30*(3), 31–58.

Elwood, S. A. (2007). Negotiating participatory ethics in the midst of institutional ethics. *ACME: An International E-Journal for Critical Geographies, 6*(3), 329–338.

Emens, E. F. (2009). Intimate discrimination: The state's role in the accidents of sex and love. *Harvard Law Review, 122,* 1307–1402.

Emens, E. F. (2014). Compulsory sexuality. *Stanford Law Review, 66*(2), 303–386.

Encarnación, O. G. (2011). Latin America's gay rights revolution. *Journal of Democracy, 22*(2), 104–118. doi:10.1353/jod.2011.0029

Epprecht, M. (2008). *Unspoken facts: A history of homosexualities in Africa.* Harare, Zimbabwe: GALZ.

Epstein, I. (2001). Using available clinical information in practice-based research: Mining for silver while dreaming of gold. *Social Work in Health Care, 33*(3/4), 15–32.

Equal Rights Trust. (2011). *The mak nyahs of Malaysia: Testimony of four transgender women* (Vol. 7). Retrieved from www.equalrightstrust.org/ertdocu mentbank/ERR7_testimony.pdf

Fawcett, B. (2009). Vulnerability: Questioning the certainties in social work and health.*InternationalSocialWork*,*52*(4),473–484.doi:10.1177/0020872809104251

Feder, E.K. (2014). *Making sense of Intersex*. Bloomington, IN: Indiana University Press.

Feigenbaum, E. (2007). Heterosexual privilege: The political and the personal. *Hypatia, 22*(1), 1–9. doi:10.1111/j.1527–2001.2007.tb01145.x

Feminist Germaine Greer sparks freedom of speech debate for views on transgender women and Caitlyn Jenner. (2015). news.com.au. Retrieved from www.news.com.au/lifestyle/real-life/news-life/feminist-germaine-greer-sparks-freedom-of-speech-debate-for-views-on-transgender-women-and-caitlyn-jenner/news-story/dd81143d20f4633527b73c9ea350e707

Fetterman, D. M., Kaftarian, S., & Wandersman, A. (2014). *Empowerment evaluation: Knowledge and tools for self-assessment, evaluation, capacity building, and accountability*. Thousand Oaks, CA: Sage.

Fiennes, C. (2013). What the first social impact bond won't tell us. *Stanford Social Innovation Review*. Retrieved from http://ssir.org/articles/entry/what_the_first_social_impact_bond_wont_tell_us

Fingerhut, A. W., Peplau, L. A., & Ghavami, N. (2005). A dual-identity framework for understanding lesbian experience. *Psychology of Women Quarterly, 29*(2), 129–139.

Finlayson, C. (2015). Review: Reflections on access: Too "vulnerable" to research. *Journal of Research in Nursing, 20*(1), 38. doi:10.1177/1744987113499519

Fischer, J. (1973). Is casework effective? A review. *Social Work, 18*(1), 5–20. doi:10.1093/sw/18.1.5

Fone, B. (2000). *Homophobia: A history*. New York: Metropolitan Books.

Forbes. (2015). *The world's billionaires*. Retrieved from www.forbes.com/billionaires/

Ford, M. E., & Kelly, P. A. (2005). Conceptualizing and categorizing race and ethnicity in health services research. *Health Services Research, 40*(5P2), 1658–1675. doi:10.1111/j.1475–6773.2005.00449.x

Foucault, M. (1978). *The history of sexuality, Volume 1: An introduction (La volunté de savoir)* (R. Hurley, Trans.). Hammondsworth, UK: Penguin (Original published in 1976).

Fouché, C. (2015). *Practice research partnerships in social work: Making a difference*. Bristol, UK: Policy Press.

Frank, A., Clough, P. T., & Seidman, S. (Eds.). (2013). *Unexpected intimacies: Moments of connection, moments of shame*. London: Routledge.

Frankowski, A. C., & Clark, L. J. (2009). Sexuality and intimacy in assisted living: Residents' perspectives and experiences. *Sexuality Research & Social Policy, 6*(4), 25–37.

Freire, P. (1970). *Pedagogy of the oppressed*. New York, NY: Herder and Herder.

Friedman, M. (2005). *Trying hard is not good enough*. Victoria, BC: Trafford Publishing.

Galinsky, M. J., Turnbull, J. E., Meglin, D. E., & Wilner, M. E. (1993). Confronting the reality of collaborative practice research: Issues of practice, design, measurement, and team development. *Social Work, 38*(4), 440–449.

Gambrill, E. D. (2003). Evidence-based practice: Sea change or the emperor's new clothes. *Journal of Social Work Education, 39*(1), 3–23.

Gambrill, E. D. (2010). Evidence-based practice and the ethics of discretion. *Journal of Social Work, 11*(1), 26–48. doi:10.1177/1468017310381306

The gap: Indigenous disadvantage in Australia. (n.d.). *Australians Together.* Retrieved from www.australianstogether.org.au/stories/detail/the-gap-indigenous-disadvantage-in-australia

Geiger, K. A., & Jordan, C. (2014). The role of societal privilege in the definitions and practices of inclusion. *Equality, Diversity and Inclusion, 33*(3), 261–274. doi:10.1108/EDI-12–2013–0115

Gert, B. (2004). *Common morality: Deciding what to do.* Oxford, UK: Oxford University Press.

Gilbert, S. G. (2006). Supplementing the traditional institutional review board with an environmental health and community review board. *Environmental Health Perspectives, 114*(10), 1626–1629. doi:10.1289/ehp.9005

Gilgun, J. E. (2005). The four cornerstones of evidence-based practice in social work. *Research in Social Work Practice, 15*(1), 52–61. doi:10.1177/1049731504269581

Gilmer, M. J., Meyer, A., Davidson, J., & Koziol-McLain, J. (2010). Staff beliefs about sexuality in aged residential care. *Nursing Praxis in New Zealand, 26*(3), 17–24.

Graham, S. (2004). It's like one of those puzzles: Conceptualising gender among bugis. *Journal of Gender Studies, 13*(2), 107–116.

Gray, M., Plath, D., & Webb, S. A. (2009). *Evidence-based social work: A critical stance.* New York, NY: Routledge.

Greenberg, D. (1988). *The construction of homosexuality.* Chicago: University of Chicago Press.

Greene, R. R., & Cohen, H. L. (2005). Social work with older adults and their families: Changing practice paradigms. *Families in Society, 86*(3), 367–373.

Greenstein, T. (2011). *The Fed's $16 trillion bailouts under-reported.* Retrieved from www.forbes.com/sites/traceygreenstein/2011/09/20/the-feds-16-trillion-bailouts-under-reported/#3246caab6877

Guillemin, M., & Gillam, L. (2004). Ethics, reflexivity, and "ethically important moments" in research. *Qualitative Inquiry, 10*(2), 261–280.

Guta, A., Nixon, S. A., & Wilson, M. G. (2013). Resisting the seduction of "ethics creep": Using Foucault to surface complexity and contradiction in research ethics review. *Social Science & Medicine, 98*(301–310). doi:10.1016/j.socscimed.2012.09.019

Gwadz, M. V., Clatt, M. C., Yi, H., Leonard, N. R., Goldsamt, L., & Lankenau, S. (2006). Resilience among young men who have sex with men in New York City. *Sexuality Research and Social Policy: Journal of NSRC, 3*(1), 13–21.

Hajjar, R. R., & Kamel, H. K. (2003). Sex and the nursing home. *Clinics in Geriatric Medicine, 19*, 575–586.

Hall, G. H., & Patrinos, H. A. (2012). *Indigenous peoples, poverty and development.* Cambridge, UK: Cambridge University Press.

Hammack, P. L. (2005). The life course development of human sexual orientation: An integrative paradigm. *Human Development, 48*(5), 267–290. doi:10.1159/000086872

Hammack, P. L., & Cohler, B. (Eds.). (2009). *The story of sexual identity: Narrative perspectives on the gay and lesbian life course.* New York, NY: Oxford University Press.

Hammersley, M. (2005). Is the evidence-based practice movement doing more harm than good? Iain Chalmers' case for research-based policy-making and practice. *Evidence and Policy, 1*(1), 85–100.

Harari, Y. N. (2011). *Sapiens: A brief history of humankind.* London: Harvill Secker.

Hastie, B., & Rimmington, D. (2014). '200 years of white affirmative action': White privilege discourse in discussions of racial inequality. *Discourse and Society, 25*(2), 186–204. doi:10.1177/0957926513516050

Hayward, L. E., Robertson, N., & Knight, C. (2012). Inappropriate sexual behaviour and dementia: An exploration of staff experiences. *Dementia, 12*(4), 463–480. doi:10.1177/1471301211434673

Henrickson, M. (2005). Can anybody work with anyone? Reframing cultural competence (Guest editorial). *Social Work Review, 17*(1), 1–2.

Henrickson, M. (2010). Civilized unions, civil rights: Same-sex relationships in Aotearoa New Zealand. *Journal of Gay & Lesbian Social Services, 21*(1/2), 40–55. doi:10.1080/10538720903332214

Henrickson, M., Neville, S., Jordan, C., & Donaghey, S. (2007). Lavender islands: The New Zealand study. *Journal of Homosexuality, 53*(4), 223–248.

Hepworth, D. H., Rooney, R. H., Rooney, G. D., & Strom-Gottfried, K. (2016). *Direct social work practice: Theory and Skills* (10th ed.). Boston, MA: Cengage.

Hewison, K., & Robison, R. (Eds.). (2006). *East Asia and the trials of neoliberalism.* Oxford, UK: Routledge.

Hicks, S. (2008). Thinking through sexuality. *Journal of Social Work, 8*(1), 65–82. doi:10.1177/1468017307084740

Higuchi, A. (2004/2014). The mechanisms of social exclusion in modern society: The dilemma of active labor market policy (trans. A. Brown). *International Journal of Japanese Sociology, 23*(1), 110–124. doi:10.1111/j.1475–6781.2012.01165.x

Hillman, J. (2008). Sexual issues and aging within the context of work with older adult patients. *Professional Psychology: Research and Practice, 39*(3), 290–297. doi:10.1037/0735-7028.39.3.290

Hiltzik, M. (2014). The NRA has blocked gun violence research for 20 years. Let's end its stranglehold on science. *Los Angeles Times.* Retrieved from www.latimes.com/business/hiltzik/la-fi-hiltzik-gun-research-funding-20160614-snap-story.html

Huffpost Entertainment. (2011). *Charlize Theron: I won't get married until my gay friends can.* Retrieved from www.huffingtonpost.com/2009/09/17/charlize-theron-i-wont-ge_n_290073.html

Hughes, C., & McCann, S. (2003). Perceived interprofessional barriers between community pharmacists and general practitioners: A qualitative assessment. *British Journal of General Practice, 53*(493), 600–606.

Hurst, S. (2008). Vulnerability in research and health care; Describing the elephant in the room? *Bioethics, 22*(4), 191–202. doi:10.1111/j.1467–8519.2008.00631.x

International Association of Schools of Social Work, & International Federation of Social Work. (2014). *Global definition of social work.* Retrieved from www.iassw-aiets.org/uploads/file/20140303_IASSW%20Website-SW%20DEFINITION%20approved%20IASSW%20Board%2021%20Jan%202014.pdf

Jay, K., & Young, A. (1977). *The gay report.* New York: Summit Books.

Jeffcott, S. A., Ibrahim, J. E., & Cameron, P. A. (2009). Resilience in healthcare and clinical handover. *BMJ Quality and Safety, 18,* 256–260. doi:10.1136/qshc.2008.030163

Jeffreys, S. (1997). Transgender activism. *Journal of Lesbian Studies, 1*(3–4), 55–74. doi:10.1300/J155v01n03_03

Jeffreys, S. (2012). The transgendering of children: Gender eugenics. *Women's Studies International Forum, 35*(5), 384–393. doi:10.1016/j.wsif.2012.07.001

Jeram, J., & Wilkinson, B. (2015). *Investing for success: Social impact bonds and the future of public services.* http://nzinitiative.org.nz/site/nzinitiative/files/Social%20Bonds%20-%20web.pdf

Jeste, D. V., & Palmer, B. W. (2013). A call for a new positive psychiatry of ageing. *British Journal of Psychiatry, 202*(2), 81–83. doi:10.1192/bjp.bp.112.110643

Johnson, J. R. (2013). Cisgender privilege, intersectionality, and the criminalization of CeCe McDonald: Why intercultural communication needs transgender studies. *Journal of International and Intercultural Communication, 6*(2), 135–144. doi:10.1080/17513057.2013.776094

Joint United Nations Programme on HIV/Acquired Immune Deficiency Syndrome. (1999). *From principle to practice: Greater involvement of people living with or affected by HIV/AIDS (GIPA).* Retrieved from http://data.unaids.org/Publications/IRC-pub01/JC252-GIPA-i_en.pdf

Jönsson, J. H. (2013). Social work beyond cultural otherisation. *Nordic Social Work Research, 3*(2), 159–167. doi:10.1080/2156857X.2013.834510

Jordan, M., Rowley, E., Morriss, R., & Manning, N. (2015). An analysis of the research team – service user relationship from the service user perspective: A consideration of 'The Three Rs'(Roles, Relations, and Responsibilities) for healthcare research organisations. *Health Expectations, 18*(6), 2693–2703. doi:10.1111/hex.12243

Kaleidoscope Trust. (2015). *Speaking out 2015: The rights of LGBTI people across the commonwealth.* http://kaleidoscopetrust.com/usr/library/documents/main/2015_speakingout_241115_web.pdf

Katz, J. N. (1996/2007). *The invention of heterosexuality.* Chicago: University of Chicago Press.

Kaufmann, J., & Wamsted, J. O. (2015). White male privilege: A conversation. *Qualitative Inquiry, 21*(1), 77–82. doi:10.1177/1077800414542695

Kemmis, S., & McTaggart, R. (2005). Communicative action and the public sphere. In N. K. Denzin & Y. S. Lincoln (Eds.), *The Sage handbook of qualitative research* (3rd ed., pp. 559–603). Thousand Oaks, CA: Sage.

Kenny, K. (2016). *Faces of innocents: Planned 'Ministry for Vulnerable Children' labelled "stigmatising" and "cripplingly disappointing".* Retrieved from www.stuff.co.nz/national/faces-of-innocents/82571122/Faces-of-Innocents-Planned-Ministry-for-Vulnerable-Children-labelled-stigmatising-and-cripplingly-disappointing

Kitzinger, C. (2005). Heteronormativity in action: Reproducing the heterosexual nuclear family in after-hours medical calls. *Social Problems, 52*(4), 477–498. doi:10.1525/sp.2005.52.4.477

Kitzinger, C., & Wilkinson, S. (1995). Transitions from heterosexuality to lesbianism: The discursive production of lesbian identities. *Developmental Psychology, 31*(1), 95–104.

Knowles, E. D., Lowery, B. S., Chow, R. M., & Unzueta, M. M. (2014). Deny, distance, or dismantle? How white Americans manage a privileged identity. *Perspectives on Psychological Science, 9*(6), 594–609. doi:10.1177/1745691614554658

Koc-Menard, N. (2015). "We are a marginal community:" The discourse of marginality in the theatre of war. *Latin American and Caribbean Ethnic Studies, 10*(2), 199–225. doi:10.1080/17442222.2015.1055890

Kottow, M. H. (2003). The vulnerable and the susceptible. *Bioethics, 17*(5–6), 460–471.

Lange, M. M., Rogers, W., & Dodds, S. (2013). Vulnerability in research ethics: A way forward. *Bioethics, 27*(6), 333–340. doi:10.1111/bioe.12032

Lee, A., Hope, T., Schmaus, J. (Producers), Lee, A. (Director). (1993). The wedding banquet. [Motion picture]. Taiwan and USA: Good Machine.

Lennox, C., Waites, M., Kirby, M., Cowell, F., Kinsman, G., Willett, G., . . . Petrova, D. (Eds.). (2013). *Human rights, sexual orientation and gender identity in the Commonwealth: Struggles for decriminalisation and change.* London, UK: Human Rights Consortium, Institute of Commonwealth Studies.

Lerner, R. M., Jacobs, F., & Wertlieb, D. (2005). *Applied developmental science: An advanced textbook.* Thousand Oaks, CA: Sage.

Leupp, G. P. (1997). *Male colors: The construction of homosexuality in Tokugawa Japan.* Berkeley, CA: University of California Press.

Leys, T., & Rodgers, G. (2015, April 22). Rayhons: "Truth finally came out" with not guilty verdict. *The Des Moines Register.* Retrieved from www.desmoinesregister.com/story/news/crime-and-courts/2015/04/22/henry-rayhons-acquitted-sexual-abuse/26105699/

Liebenberg, L., & Ungar, M. (2009). Introduction: The challenge of researching resilience. In L. Liebenber & M. Ungar (Eds.), *Researching resilience* (pp. 3–25). Toronto: University of Toronto Press.

Little, P., Everitt, H., Williamson, I., Warner, G., Moore, M., Gould, C., . . . Payne, S. (2001). Preferences of patients for patient centred approach to consultation in primary care: Observational study. *British Medical Journal, 322*, 1–7.

Lowes, R. (2014). *AMA to Congress: Lift ban on CDC gun research.* Retrieved from www.medscape.com/viewarticle/864797

Luna, F. (2009). Elucidating the concept of vulnerability: Layers not labels. *International Journal of Feminist Approaches to Bioethics, 2*, 121–139.

Luna, F. (2014). "Vulnerability," an interesting concept for public health: The case of older persons. *Public Health Ethics, 7*(2), 180–194. doi:10.1093/phe/phu012

McCormack, B. (2003). A conceptual framework for person-centred practice with older people. *International Journal of Nursing Practice, 9,* 202–209.

McIntosh, M. (1986). The homosexual role. *Social Problems, 16*(2), 182–192.

Mackenzie, S. (2013). *Structural intimacies: Sexual stories in the Black AIDS epidemic.* New Brunswick, NJ: Rutgers University Press.

Makofane, K. (2012). Unspoken facts: A history of homosexualities in Africa. *Culture, Health & Sexuality, 15*(Sup 1), 114–116. doi:10.1080/13691058.201 2.738149

Malagón-Oviedo, R. A., & Czeresnia, D. (2015). The concept of vulnerability and its biosocial nature. *Interface (Botucatu), 19*(53), 237–249.

Mallon, G. P. (Ed.). (2008). *Social work practice with lesbian, gay, bisexual and transgender people* (2nd ed.). New York: Routledge.

Martin, A. K., Tavaglione, N., & Hurst, S. (2014). Resolving the conflict: Clarifying "vulnerability" in health care ethics. *Kennedy Institute of Ethics Journal, 24*(1), 51–72. doi:10.1353/ken.2014.0005

Martin, D. G. (2007). Bureacratizing ethics: Institutional review boards and participatory research. *ACME: An International E-Journal for Critical Geographies, 6*(3), 319–328.

Martin, F., Jackson, P. A., McLelland, M., & Yue, A. (Eds.). (2008). *AsiaPacifiQueer: Rethinking genders and sexualities.* Urbana: University of Illinois.

Martin, J. (2016). The death of neoliberalism and the crisis in western politics. *The Guardian.* Retrieved from www.theguardian.com/commentisfree/2016/aug/21/death-of-neoliberalism-crisis-in-western-politics?CMP=fb_gu

Matthews, S. (2011). Becoming African: Debating post-apartheid White South African identities. *Africa Identities, 9*(1), 1–17. doi:10.1080/14725843.2011. 530440

Mayan, M. J., & Daum, C. (2015). Beyond dissemination: Generating and applying qualitative evidence through community-based participatory research. In K. Olson, R. A. Young, & I. Z. Schultz (Eds.), *Handbook of qualitative health research for evidence-based practice* (Vol. 4, pp. 441–452). New York, NY: Springer.

Miers, M. (2010). Learning for new ways of working. In K. D. Pollard, J. Thomas, & M. Miers (Eds.), *Understanding interprofessional working in health and social care: Theory and practice* (pp. 74–89). Basingstoke, UK: Palgrave Macmillan.

Mills, C. W. (1956). *The power elite.* New York: Oxford University Press.

Ministry of Social Development. (n.d.). Investing in services for outcomes. Retrieved from www.msd.govt.nz/about-msd-and-our-work/work-programmes/investing-in-services-for-outcomes/index.html

Mohanty, J., & Newhill, C. E. (2011). Asian adolescent and young adult adoptees' psychological well-being: Examining the mediating role of marginality. *Children and Youth Services Review, 33*(7), 1189–1195. doi:10.1016/j.childyouth.2011.02.016

Montgomery, S. A., & Stewart, A. J. (2012). Privileged allies in lesbian and gay rights activism: Gender, generation and resistance to heteronormativity. *Journal of Social Issues, 68*(1), 162–177. doi:10.1111/j.1540-4560.2012.01742.x

Moore, T., Noble-Carr, D., & McArthur, M. (2016). Changing things for the better: The use of children and young people's reference groups in social research. *International Journal of Social Research Methodology, 19*(2), 241–256. doi:10 .1080/13645579.2014.989640

Morgan, S., & Yoder, L. (2012). A concept analysis of person-centred care. *Journal of Holistic Nursing, 30*(1), 6–15. doi:10.1177/0898010111412189

Munford, R., & Sanders, J. (2003). *Making a difference in families: Research that creates change.* Crow's Nest, NSW, Australia: Allen & Unwin.

Murray, S. O. (2002). *Pacific homosexualities.* San José, CA: Writers Club Press.

Murray, S. O., & Roscoe, W. (Eds.). (1997). *Islamic homosexualities: Culture, history and literature.* New York: New York University Press.

National Commission for the Protection of Human Subjects of Biomedical and Behavioral Research. (1979). *The Belmont report: Ethical principles and guidelines for the protection of human subjects of research.* www.hhs.gov/ohrp/ regulations-and-policy/belmont-report/#

New Zealand Ethics Committee (n.d.). *New Zealand ethics committee.* Retrieved from www.nzethics.com/

Nicholson, L. (2013). Let me tell you who I am: Intimacy, privacy and self-disclosure. In A. Frank, P. T. Clough, & S. Seidman (Eds.), *Intimacies: A new world of relational life* (pp. 30–46). London: Routledge.

Noble, C., & Henrickson, M. (2014). Towards identifying a philosophical basis for social work. In C. Noble, H. Strauss, & B. Littlechild (Eds.), *Global social work: Crossing borders, blurring boundaries* (pp. 3–14). Sydney, NSW: Sydney University Press.

NoiseCat, J. B. (2015). *13 issues facing native people beyond mascots and casinos.* Retrieved from www.huffingtonpost.com/entry/13-native-american-issues_us_55b7d801e4b0074ba5a6869c

Nuremburg Code. (1949). *Trials of war criminals before the Nuremberg military tribunals under Control Council Law No. 10.* Washington, DC: U.S. Government Printing Office. Retrieved from https://history.nih.gov/research/downloads/ nuremberg.pdf

O'Brien, M. (2016). The triplets: Investment in outcomes for the vulnerable: Reshaping social services for (some) New Zealand children. *Aotearoa New Zealand Social Work Review, 28*(2), 9–21.

Open Society Foundations. (2012). *Criminalising condoms: How policing practices put sex workers and HIV services at risk in Kenya, Namibia, Russia, South Africa, the United States, and Zimbabwe.* Retrieved from www.opensociety foundations.org/reports/criminalizing-condoms

Ostry, J. D., Lougani, P. L., & Furceri, D. (2016). Neoliberalism: Oversold? *Finance & Development, 53*(2). Retrieved from International Monetary Fund: www.imf.org/external/pubs/ft/fandd/2016/06/ostry.htm

Oswin, N. (2010). The modern model family at home in Singapore: A queer geography. *Transactions of the Institute of British Geographers, 35*(2), 256–268. doi:10.1111/j.1475–5661.2009.00379.x

Ott, M. A. (2014). Vulnerability in HIV prevention research with adolescents, reconsidered. *Journal of Adolescent Health*, *54*(6), 629–630. doi:10.1016/j. jadohealth.2014.03.014

Owen, D. (2013). Citizenship and the marginalities of migrants. *Critical Review of International Social and Political Philosophy*, *16*(3), 326–343. doi:10.1080/ 13698230.2013.795702

Oxfam. (2016). *An economy for the 1%*. Oxford, UK. Retrieved from https:// www.oxfam.org/en/research/economy-1

Paolillo, J. (2005). Language diversity on the Internet. In UNESCO Institute for Statistics (Ed.), *Measuring linguistic diversity on the Internet*. Montreal: UNESCO. Retrieved from https://pdfs.semanticscholar.org/761d/9e2168dc206ecc9 61640289e7275d1d5b32b.pdf

Parent, M. C., DeBlaere, C., & Moradi, B. (2013). Approaches to research on intersectionality: Perspectives on gender, LGBT, and racial/ethnic identities. *Sex Roles*, *68*(11–12), 639–645. doi:10.1007/s11199-013-0283-2

Park, A. (2014). *10 Supreme Court rulings that turned corporations into people*. Retrieved from www.alternet.org/10-supreme-court-rulings-turned-corporations-people

Park, R. E. (1928). Human migration and the marginal man. *American Journal of Sociology*, *33*(6), 881–893.

Patton, M. Q. (2011). *Developmental evaluation: Applying complexity concepts to enhance innovation and use*. New York, NY: Guilford Press.

Payne, M. (2005). *Modern social work theory*. Basingstoke, UK: Palgrave Macmillan.

Plummer, K. (1995). *Telling sexual stories: Power, change and social worlds*. London: Routledge.

Poindexter, C., & Shippy, A. (2008). Networks of older New Yorkers with HIV: Fragility, resilience and transformation. *AIDS Patient Care and STIs*, *22*(9), 723–733.

Pollard, K. C., Thomas, J., & Miers, M. (Eds.). (2010). *Understanding interprofessional working in health and social care: Theory and practice*. Basingstoke, UK: Palgrave Macmillan.

Pols, R. G., Battersby, M. W., Regan-Smith, M., Markwick, M. J., Lawrence, J., Auret, K., . . . Nguyen, H. (2009). Chronic condition self-management support: Proposed competencies for medical students. *Chronic Illness*, *5*(7), 7–14.

Press, E. (2015, May 2). Madness. *New Yorker*, *92*, 38–47.

Price, E. (2012). Gay and lesbian carers: Ageing in the shadow of dementia. *Ageing and Society*, *32*(3), 516–532.

ProPublica. (2016). *Bailout recipients*. Retrieved from https://projects.propublica. org/bailout/list

Quinlivan, K., Rasmussen, M. L., Aspin, C., Allen, L., & Sanjakdar, F. (2014). Crafting the normative subject: Queerying the politics of race in the New Zealand Health education classroom. *Discourse*, *35*(3), 393–404. doi:10.1080/015 96306.2014.888843

Rahman, Q., & Wilson, G. D. (2003). Born gay? The psychobiology of human sexual orientation. *Personality and Individual Differences, 34*(8), 1337–1382.

Reason, P., & Bradbury, H. (Eds.). (2008). *The Sage handbook of action research: Participative inquiry and practice* (2nd ed.). London, UK: Sage.

Reed, J. (2007). *Appreciative inquiry: Research for change*. London, UK: Sage.

Rich, A. (1980/1986). Compulsory heterosexuality and lesbian existence. In A. Rich (Ed.), *Blood, bread and poetry* (pp. 23–75). London: Virago.

Rogers, C. R. (1961). *On becoming a person: A therapist's view of psychotherapy*. Boston: Houghton Mifflin.

Rosowsky, E. (2009). Challenge and resilience in old age. *Generations: Journal of the American Society on Aging, 33*(3), 100–102.

Rossi, P. H., Lipsey, M. W., & Freeman, H. E. (2004). *Evaluation: A systematic approach* (7th ed.). Thousand Oaks, CA: Sage.

Rubin, A. T. (2011). Punitive penal preferences and support for welfare: Applying the "goverance of social marginality" thesis to the individual level. *Punishment & Society, 13*(2), 198–229. doi:10.1177/1462474510394960

Russell, S. T., Clarke, T. J., & Clary, J. (2009). Are teens "post-gay"? Contemporary adolescents' sexual identity labels. *Journal of Youth and Adolescence, 38*(7), 884–890.

Saleebey, D. (Ed.) (2002). *The strengths perspective in social work practice*. Boston, MA: Allyn & Bacon.

Sang, T.-I. D. (2003). *The emerging lesbian: Female same-sex desire in modern China*. Chicago: University of Chicago Press.

Savage, M. (2014). *Paula Bennett wastes taxpayers money on drug testing*. Retrieved from http://thestandard.org.nz/paula-bennett-wastes-taxpayers-money-on-drug-testing/

Savedoff, W., & Madan, J. (2015). *A social impact bond without the impact? Critics question success of early childhood development program*. Retrieved from www.cgdev.org/blog/social-impact-bond-without-impact-critics-question-success-early-childhood-development-program

Savin-Williams, R. C. (2005). *The new gay teenager*. Cambridge, MA: Harvard University Press.

Schäfer, M., Haun, D. B. M., & Tomasello, M. (2015). Fair is not fair everywhere. *Psychological Science, 26*(8), 1252–1260. doi:10.1177/0956797615586188

Scheman, N. (2014). Empowering canaries: Sustainability, vulnerability and the ethics of epistemology. *The International Journal of Feminist Approaches to Bioethics, 7*(1), 169–191. doi:10.1353/ijf.2014.0002

Schmidt, J. (2001). Redefining fa'afafine: Western discourses and the construction of transgenderism in Samoa. *Intersections*, (6). Retrieved from http://intersections.anu.edu.au/issue6/schmidt.html

Schouten, V. (2015). *Explaining the wrong of rape* (PhD dissertation), Princeton, Ann Arbor, MI.

Scott, V. M., Mottarella, K. E., & Lavooy, M. (2006). Does virtual intimacy exist? A brief exploration into reported levels of intimacy in online relationships. *Cyberpsychology and Behavior, 9*(6), 759–761.

Sedgwick, E. K. (1990). *Epistemology of the closet*. Berkeley, CA: University of California Press.

Seidman, S. (2013). State and class politics in the making of a culture of intimacy. In A. Frank, P. T. Clough, & S. Seidman (Eds.), *Intimacies: A new world of relational life* (pp. 13–29). London: Routledge.

Semali, L. M., & Shakespeare, E. S. (2014). Rethinking mindscapes and symbols of patriarchy in the workforce to explain gendered privileges and rewards. *International Education Studies, 7*(2), 37–53. doi:10.5539/ies.v7n2p37

Shaw, I. (2005). Practitioner research: Evidence or critique? *British Journal of Social Work, 35*(8), 1231–1248. doi:10.1093/bjsw/bch223

Shin, H. (2015). Everyday racism in Canadian schools: Ideologies of language and culture among Korean transnational students in Toronto. *Journal of Multilingual and Multicultural Development, 36*(1), 67–79. doi:10.1080/01434632.2014.892502

Shore, N. (2007). Re-conceptualizing the Belmont Report: A community-based participatory research perspective. *Journal of Community Practice, 14*(4), 5–26. doi:10.1300/J125v14n04_02

Shuttleworth, R., Russell, C., Weerakoon, P., & Dune, T. (2010). Sexuality in residential aged care: A survey of perceptions and policies in Australian nursing homes. *Sexuality and Disability, 28*(3), 187–194. doi:10.1007/s11195-010-9164-6

Simon, W., & Gagnon, J. (1973/2009). *Sexual conduct: The social sources of human sexuality* (2nd ed.). New Brunswick, NJ: Aldine Transaction.

Smith, L. T. (2008). On tricky ground: Researching the native. In N. K. Denzin & Y. S. Lincoln (Eds.), *The Sage handbook of qualitative research* (3rd ed., pp. 113–143). Thousand Oaks, CA: Sage.

Soklaridis, S., Oandasan, I., & Kimpton, S. (2007). Family health teams: Can health professionals learn to work together? *Canadian Family Physician, 53*(7), 1198–1199.

Solomon, A. (2012). *Far from the tree: parents, children and the search for identity*. New York: Scribner.

Sorell, T. (2016). Law and equity in Hobbes. *Critical Review of International Social and Political Philosophy, 19*(1), 29–46. doi:10.1080/13698260.2015.1122353

Statistics New Zealand. (n.d.). *New Zealand's prison population*. Retrieved from www.stats.govt.nz/browse_for_stats/snapshots-of-nz/yearbook/society/crime/corrections.aspx

Stringer, E. T. (2014). *Action research* (3rd ed.). London, UK: Sage.

Sue, D. W. (Ed.). (2010). *Microaggressions and marginality*. Hoboken, NJ: John Wiley & Sons.

Tabak, N., & Shemesh-Kigli, R. (2006). Sexuality and Alzheimer's disease: Can the two go together? *Nursing Forum, 41*(4), 158–166.

Tadele, G. (2011). Heteronormativity and 'troubled' masculinities among men who have sex with men in Addis Ababa. *Culture, Health and Sexuality, 13*(4), 457–469.

Tait, M. (2015). *Patients, not prisoners: New system for mentally ill.* Retrieved from www.nzherald.co.nz/nz/news/article.cfm?c_id=1&objectid=11562233

Teich, N. M. (2012). *Transgender 101: A simple guide to a complex issue.* New York, NY: Columbia University Press.

Thórarinsdóttir, K., & Kristjánsson, K. (2012). Patients' perspectives on person-centred participation in healthcare: A framework analysis. *Nursing Ethics.* doi:10.1177/0969733013490593

Thyer, B. A. (2004). What is evidence-based practice? *Brief Treatment and Crisis Intervention, 4*(2), 167–176.

Tin, L.-G. (2008/2012). *The invention of heterosexual culture.* Cambridge, MA: MIT Press.

Todd, N. R., McConnell, E. A., & Suffrin, R. L. (2014). The role of attitudes toward white privilege and religious beliefs in predicting social justice interest and commitment. *American Journal of Community Psychology, 53*(1–2), 109–121. doi:10.1007/s10464-014–9630-x

Tonn, S. (2014). *Stanford research suggests support for incarceration mirrors whites' perception of black prison populations.* Retrieved from http://news.stanford.edu/news/2014/august/prison-black-laws-080614.html

Underwood, C. (2014). *72% of the indigenous population in Mexico live in extreme poverty conditions.* Retrieved from www.theyucatantimes.com/2014/08/72-of-the-indigenous-population-in-mexico-live-in-extreme-poverty-conditions

United Nations Educational Scientific and Cultural Organisation [UNESCO]. (2006). *Universal declaration on bioethics and human rights.* United Nations. Retrieved from http://unesdoc.unesco.org/images/0014/001461/146180E.pdf

UN Water. (2013). UN Water World Water Day. Retrieved from www.unwater.org/water-cooperation-2013/water-cooperation/facts-and-figures/en

Usage of content languages for websites. (2016). W3Techs. Retrieved from http://w3techs.com/technologies/overview/content_language/all

Vanita, R. (Ed.). (2002). *Queering India: Same-sex love and eroticism in Indian culture and society.* New York: Routledge.

Villar, F., Celdrán, M., Fabà, J., & Serrat, R. (2014). Staff attitudes towards sexual relationships among institutionalized people with dementia: Does an extreme cautionary stance predominate? *International Psychogeriatrics, 26*(3), 403–412. doi:10.1017/s1044640213002342

Vitiello, G. (2011). *The libertine's friend: Homosexuality and masculinity in late imperial China.* Chicago: University of Chicago Press.

Vulnerable Children Act 2014, Pub. L. No. 2014 No. 40 (2014 30 June 2014).

Wacquant, L. (2004/2009). *Punishing the poor.* Durham, NC: Duke University Press.

Wacquant, L. (2010). Crafting the neoliberal state: Workfare, prisonfare, and social insecurity. *Sociological Forum, 25*(2), 197–220. doi:10.1111/j.1573-7861.2010.01173.x

Wagner, E. H., Austin, B. T., Davis, C., Hindmarsh, M., Schaefer, J., & Bonomi, A. (2001). Improving chronic illness care: Translating evidence into action. *Health Affairs, 20*(6), 64–78.

Walters, I. (2006). *Country report: Vietnam*. Retrieved from www.transgenderasia. org/country_report_vietnam.htm

Wang, L. I. (2004). Race as proxy: Situational racism and self-fulfilling stereotypes. *DePaul Law Review, 53*, 1013–1109.

Ward, J. (2015). *Not gay: Sex between straight white men*. New York: New York University Press.

Webb, S. A. (2001). Some considerations on the validity of evidence-based practice in social work. *British Journal of Social Work, 31*(1), 57–79.

Weeks, J. (2009). *Sexuality* (3rd ed.). London: Routledge.

Werner, E. (2005). Resilience research. In R. Peters, B. Leadbeater, & R. McMahon (Eds.), *Resilience in children, families and communities* (pp. 3–12). New York: Kluwer Academic/Plenum Publishers.

Wilkerson, J. M., Ross, M. W., & Brooks, A. K. (2009). Social constructions influencing sociosexual identity development of collegiate gay and bisexual men. *Sexuality Research and Social Policy, 6*(2), 71–87.

Wilkinson, A., & Whitehead, L. (2009). Evolution of the concept of self-care and implications for nurses: A literature review. *International Journal of Nursing Studies, 46*, 1143–1147.

Windle, G. (2011). What is resilience? A review and concept analysis. *Reviews in Clinical Gerontology, 21*(2), 152–169. doi:10.1017/S0959259810000420

Winter, S., & Udomsak, N. (2002). Male, female and transgender: Stereotypes and self in Thailand. *International Journal of Transgenderism, 6*(1). Retrieved from http://www.transgenderasia.org/paper_male_female.htm

Witham, G., Beddow, A., & Haigh, C. (2015). Reflections on access: Too vulnerable to research? *Journal of Research in Nursing, 20*(1), 28–37. doi:10. 1177/1744987113499338

Wolf, L. E. (2010). The research ethics committee is not the enemy: Oversight of community-based participatory research. *Journal of Empirical Research on Human Research Ethics, 5*(4), 77–86. doi:10.1525/jer.2010.5.4.77

Wood, K. M. (1978). Casework effectiveness: A new look at the research evidence. *Social Work, 23*(6), 437–458.

World Bank. (2015). *Access to electricity (% of population)*. Retrieved from http://data.worldbank.org/indicator/EG.ELC.ACCS.ZS

World Medical Association. (1964/2013). *Declaration of Helsinki: Ethical principles for medical research involving human subjects*. Retrieved from www.wma. net/en/30publications/10policies/b3/

Young, I. M. (1990). *Justice and the politics of difference*. Princeton, NJ: Princeton University Press.

Zufferey, C. (2013). "Not knowing that I do not know and not wanting to know:" Reflections of a white Australian social worker. *International Social Work, 56*(5), 659–673. doi:10.1177/0020872812436624

Index

Page numbers in *italic* indicate a figure or table on the corresponding page.